I Saw a Pale Horse
AND SELECTED POEMS FROM
Diary of a Vagabond

I Saw a Pale Horse
(Aouma wo mitari)

AND SELECTED POEMS FROM Diary of a Vagabond
(Hōrōki)

Hayashi Fumiko

INTRODUCTION AND TRANSLATION BY
Janice Brown

East Asia Program
Cornell University
Ithaca, New York 14853

The Cornell East Asia Series is published by the Cornell University East Asia Program and has no formal affiliation with Cornell University Press. We are a small, non-profit press, publishing reasonably-priced books on a wide variety of scholarly topics relating to East Asia as a service to the academic community and the general public. We accept standing orders which may be cancelled at any time and which provide for automatic billing and shipping of each title in the series upon publication.

If after review by internal and external readers a manuscript is accepted for publication, it is published on the basis of camera-ready copy provided by the volume author. Each author is thus responsible for any necessary copy-editing and for manuscript formatting. Submission inquiries should be addressed to Editorial Board, East Asia Program, Cornell University, Ithaca, New York 14853-7601.

Photo p. ii courtesy of Janice Brown

Number 86 in the Cornell East Asia Series
AOUMA WO MITARI by Fumiko Hayashi
Copyright © 1951 by Fukue Hayashi
HOROKI by Fumiko Hayashi
Copyright © 1951 by Fukue Hayashi
English translation rights arranged with Nihon Bungei Chosakuken Hogo Domei through Janice Brown/Japan Foreign-Rights Centre
English language translation copyright © 1997 Janice Brown
ISSN 1050-2955
ISBN 1-885445-86-5 paper
ISBN 1-885445-66-0 cloth
Printed in the United States of America

In memory

Robert Lucas

Contents

Acknowledgements

My incentive to read the works of Hayashi Fumiko came initially from Professor Kinya Tsuruta of the University of British Columbia, who first suggested I undertake a reading of Fumiko's texts. Owing to Professor Tsuruta's assistance and eminent scholarly advice in the preparation of my dissertation on Fumiko's major writings, I set upon a path that led eventually from Hayashi Fumiko into the wide world of Japanese female writing. Years later, on a bright spring morning in May, strolling along the *Bungaku no Komichi* (Literature Way) above the town of Onomichi, I had further opportunity to reflect upon my choice. Coming upon a familiar quotation from Hayashi Fumiko's *Hōrōki* included among some twenty-five poetic inscriptions incised on various commemorative stones, I became suddenly aware of the richness of Fumiko's art and of her singular accomplishment in Japanese poetry. If anything, that springtime walk led me to read more of Fumiko's poetry and eventually to embark upon this translation.

Expressions of gratitude are also due to Professor Isogai Hideo of Hiroshima for his support and guidance while I was a graduate student at the University of British Columbia and also during the time I spent in Japan. Professor Isogai's extensive knowledge of Japanese literature, in particular the life and writings of Hayashi Fumiko, made him an excellent and invaluable mentor. I would also like to convey my heartfelt appreciation to Dr. Tomone Matsumoto, also of Hiroshima, for her careful reading of the translations against the original *Aouma wo mitari*, and also to Tomoko Fujiwara of Kyoto for her initial comments upon Fumiko's text. Dr. Michiko Kawashima of the University of Alberta was also of great assistance, giving freely of her time and effort in attempts to answer my numerous questions connected with Fumiko's poetic texts. Further, I would like to offer a very special thanks to my colleague in Japanese literature, Dr. Sonja Arntzen of the University of Alberta, for her advice, encouragement, and enthusiastic reading of the manuscript.

I would also like to mention those friends to whom I am much indebted for advice and unfailing support during the time I spent in Japan researching material for this book. I would like to acknowledge especially the kind assistance of Professor and Mrs. Toyobu Watanabe, Hiromi and Naomi Okunishi, and Judith Clancy, all of Kyoto.

Some of the information on Hayashi Fumiko's early life has appeared previously in *Japan Quarterly*, January-March, 1996, entitled "Voice from the Margin: Hayashi Fumiko," and is reprinted here with Japan Quarterly's kind permission. Also, the front cover of Yosano Akiko's *Midaregami* is reproduced by permission of Nihon Kindai Bungakukan. Acknowledgement is due also to the Hayashi estate and to the services of the Japan Foreign-Rights Centre for permission to publish these translations of Fumiko's poetry. I would further like to extend my thanks and appreciation to the managing editor of the Cornell East Asia Series, Karen Smith, for her invaluable advice in all the many details of publication and to the anonymous reader for his or her most helpful suggestions with the manuscript. Finally, in the preparation of this manuscript for publication, I would like to express my sincere gratitude for the competent and efficient services of Heather McDonald. Without her expertise in the intricacies of word-processing and formatting, this book would not have taken its present shape.

Last but certainly not least, I would like to express my gratitude and appreciation to my husband, William, and to my daughters, Shelina and Sylvan, for their patience and support during the time taken to complete this project.

Part I

Introduction

"These days . . . no one delves deeply into poetry. I feel as if we have forgotten something important."

Hayashi Fumiko.

Near a busy railway station in the Japanese seaside town of Onomichi stands the bronze statue of a woman. Old-fashioned wicker case and umbrella at her side, one hand raised thoughtfully to her chin, the life-size, kimono-clad figure squats on her heels, a traveller resting briefly on a journey. From the inscription on the broad pedestal that supports this oddly intent figure, passers-by learn that this is a likeness of the writer, Hayashi Fumiko (1903-1951). This statue of Fumiko, an exception in a country where statues of male leaders and heroes predominate, is extraordinary not only in that it represents a female figure but also that it memorializes a writing woman who spoke from the margins of society, who gave voice to the underprivileged, the impoverished, the dispossessed, who dared sing of her life as a poor and working-class woman.[1] Erected in 1984, the Fumiko statue represents a rare popular tribute to this unconventional writer whose colorful poetry, essays, and prose fiction established her as one of the most important women writers of twentieth-century Japanese literature.

Onomichi, the town Fumiko came to call home, has acquired over the years something of a reputation as a minor literary and cultural mecca, a "little Kyoto," as the guidebooks would have it. Some visitors come for the old temples that dot the hillsides. Some come to wander the picturesque harbor area. Still others come to follow the "literary pathways" that wind through the steep streets above the town. On those narrow, cobbled by-ways, the tourist may visit a variety of sights associated with Fumiko, with the writer Shiga Naoya (1883-1971), the

1

tanka poet Nakamura Kenkichi (1889-1934), and other writers and artists who over the course of time have made their way to this remote corner of Japan. The Fumiko statue, however, is the most prominent of these literary landmarks, and most of the travellers who pass through the Onomichi station pause at the Fumiko bronze to read the inscription: "I have seen the sea. I can see thé sea. The sea at Onomichi which I haven't seen for five years. How nostalgic it makes me feel!"[2] Many have their photograph taken beside the bronze figure, and none seem surprised to find Fumiko's likeness in such a bustling, inelegant spot. The roadside, the railway station, the cheap lodging house—locales such as these are popularly known to have sparked Fumiko's creative energies and set her on the road to literary success. Marginal areas of human existence gave rise not only to Fumiko's own distinctive literature but also have become inextricably linked in the popular imagination with Fumiko's image as a writer and a woman. Rather than a quiet temple or an isolated grove on the hillside, the ebb and flow of the unceasing Onomichi human traffic seems an appropriate setting in which to honor a writer who drew her inspiration from the lives of ordinary people, who spent most of her life on the move, and who did not hesitate to proclaim herself publicly as a writing and speaking woman.

The 'Forgotten' Poet

Although Fumiko has long been recognized as a talented writer of *shōsetsu*, or prose fiction, her earliest writings in poetry have been all but ignored. In fact, Fumiko was a poet of considerable genius. Yet today only one poem by Fumiko is popularly remembered: *hana no inochi wa mijikakute nigishiki koto no mi ōkariki*[3] (A flower's life is brief, its painful sufferings many). Oft-quoted, its tough sentimentality has become part of Japan's commonly held literary heritage. In its brevity, however, this verse can do little more than suggest the poetic sub-stratum that underlies Fumiko's writings; there is little indication of the depth and significance of that hidden layer. Rather than illuminating Fumiko's buried poetic past, *hana no inochi wa* has come to be associated simply with the projected persona of Hayashi Fumiko herself, outcast woman writer who battled great odds to achieve success but who never won acceptance or true happiness. Her poetry outside of this one iconic poem remains today largely unexamined.

While the annals of Shōwa (1925-1988) literary history are strangely silent on matters to do with Fumiko the poet, Japanese scholars have begun recently to re-evaluate Fumiko's early poetry texts, including the first poetry collection, *I Saw a Pale Horse* (*Aouma wo mitari*, 1929), and other poetry from her *Diary of a Vagabond* (*Hōrōki*, 1928-1930).[4] Some indication of the reasons for the earlier undervaluation of Fumiko have emerged from these studies, not least of which is the issue of gender. Thus, Mori Eiichi, in his recent study of Fumiko's texts, questions the canonical status of anarcho-dadaist poets writing at the same time as Fumiko: "Today, as I read over some of these poets' works, have any of these poets managed to endure? The poems of Hayashi Fumiko . . . shine more brightly by far."[5] Comparing Fumiko to male poets, such as Shimazaki Tōson (1872-1943), Murō Saisei (1889-1962), Nakano Shigeharu (1902-1979), Hori Tatsuo (1904-1953) and others, another critic points out that "(Fumiko) is by no means inferior."[6] Fumiko, the vagabond poet, who in life tirelessly took her manuscripts from door to door, would no doubt be exceedingly pleased, perhaps even surprised, at this chance for new readings. Thus, even though it is still common in Japan to privilege male poets and writers of the modern period over female, women's texts *are* being read and, increasingly, as in the case of Fumiko, recuperated by present-day scholars. While tendencies towards gender discrimination in the literary field have been ameliorated somewhat in recent times, the Japanese literary establishment in the 1920s, the period in which Fumiko first began to write, was not hospitable to women, and perhaps as a result of that bias, even today, it is rare to find literary historical studies that include discussions of women poets of this era.[7]

Another factor cited as contributing to Fumiko's omission from poetry histories is her highhanded treatment of fellow poets once she had achieved literary eminence with *Diary of a Vagabond*. The most often mentioned incident concerns Fumiko's refusal to answer the door when acquaintances from her anarchist days came calling.[8] One critic, Tōmaru Tatsu, speculates that Fumiko's estrangement from her former colleagues and associates may have been one reason why her poetry came to be undervalued and nearly erased from inclusion in histories of poetry circles.[9] Reading the comments and recollections of Fumiko's colleagues today, I would argue also that beneath the ire and resentment Fumiko's cavalier treatment of her old friends aroused lies more than a hint of jealousy. Certainly, such success as fell to Fumiko was never enjoyed, even remotely, by those who came to castigate her.

Reading Fumiko's poetry as 'forgotten' (or, as Tōmaru would have it, "buried") also connects Fumiko's poetry with issues of class as well as gender and personality. Tōmaru points out that Fumiko's extreme independence, her preference for "stick(ing) to her lone position,"[10] and not participating in the poetry *bundan* as further causes for her lack of recognition by poetry circles. In fact, Fumiko was not accepted by any literary group, establishment or anti-establishment, male or female. Unable to claim the education and upbringing accorded some of her female colleagues, such as Miyamoto Yuriko (1899-1951) and Enchi Fumiko (1905-1986), or to demonstrate the intellectual achievement and/or ideological commitment of Miyamoto, Sata Ineko (1904-), and Hirabayashi Taiko (1905-1971), Fumiko remained an outcast among female writers, a *lumpen proletariat*, who could only write her desire of the center—the fine world of pianos, suburban skies, beautiful autumn clothes, freshly baked bread—yet never truly possess it. When eventually she acquired the wherewithal to buy her way in, the center remained ever elusive, Fumiko labelled a *nouveau riche*.

At the same time, however, Fumiko's own writing practice led to the undervaluation of her poetry. Early in her career, soon after the publication of the best-selling *Diary of a Vagabond*, Fumiko made the decision to abandon poetry in favour of prose. It goes without saying that a number of Japanese writers of prose also write poetry, yet there are few who win recognition for accomplishments in both areas. Generally, the two genres remain single pursuits. Fumiko, however, in spite of her initial success as a poet, determined to master *shōsetsu*, and in this she was eventually and eminently successful. Fumiko's poetry, overshadowed and superseded, became a relatively minor element in the construction of her prose texts. Literary scholars began to treat her poetic career as but one element in her biographical chronology and viewed her poetic writing merely as a developmental 'stage' in her overall growth as a writer. This, as much as the other considerations noted above, seems to have effectively discouraged attempts at examining Fumiko's poetic writings until recently when re-readings of non-canonical texts, such as Fumiko's, began to be undertaken.

Opening the pages of *I Saw a Pale Horse* is thus to enter *terra incognita*—the unknown poetic world of a young Japanese female poet writing at a time when women were all but excluded from the centers of literary production, when the poet herself had only begun to construct the female subject that would later become the central figure of her entire opus. On the threshold of success, one year before her *Diary of a Vagabond* became a national best-seller, the poet gathered together some of her favorite poems, arranged them in a collection, borrowed the publication fees, and published her work. The front cover offers a provocative design: a seated female figure in silhouette, the protruding breast more than hinting at nudity. The somatic image is appropriate to the text, as we ascertain from the reactions of one of Fumiko's contemporaries, the writer, Enchi Fumiko . In a short review of Fumiko's first poetry collection, Enchi remarks: "I feel your nude figure . . . I feel your eyes, your mouth, your nose, your ears, your arms and legs, I feel your entire body in every part (of your work)."[11] For Enchi, Fumiko's poems are read as a kind of organic self-writing, in which the body of the poet is also the body of the text.

The corporeal impact of Fumiko's poems is further acknowledged in other critical evaluations. Fellow writer, female friend, and later biographer of Fumiko, Hirabayashi Taiko describes Hayashi's poems as " . . . carved . . . in painful characters bathed in blood."[12] In a more recent assessment (1984), male poet and critic, Tōmaru Tatsu, likens his first reading of *I Saw a Pale Horse* to "being hit over the head with an axe."[13] While Tōmaru's remark is extreme, his reaction registers recognition of Fumiko's poetry as singularly aggressive, a text that literally assaults the reader. Enchi and Hirabayashi also take note of this presence, but view it in terms of overwhelming physicality (Enchi) or as an expression of violent emotional intensity (Hirabayashi). In general, Fumiko's textual persona seems surprisingly demanding for readers of both genders and of widely divergent eras.

Fumiko's decision to write her female subject as carnal, or as *incarnated* in the female body, is to a great extent in keeping with Japanese women's literary practice. Female poets, from ninth century Ono no Komachi to twentieth century Yosano Akiko (1878-1942), have celebrated female desire. Akiko was the first to introduce hitherto unwritten images of the female body into modern Japanese poetic discourse. Nonetheless, the full body of the seated nude form on the cover of *I Saw a Pale Horse* is distinct in both form and spirit from the entwining foliate complexity of the female profile on Akiko's first poetry collection, *Tangled Hair* (*Midaregami*, 1901). Suggestive and alluring, the sinuous tracings of Akiko's inscription evoke a female image that is both sensuous and seductive—an art nouveau rendering that bespeaks its times. Fumiko's cover, too, is marked by its own contemporaneity, the spare, linear art deco composition jutting out uncompromisingly into the graphic space. Yet, there is another aspect of the Fumiko design that adds to its impact. The seated female figure, viewed from another angle of perception, might also be perceived as the sharp-angled profile of a female head; in this case, the protruding breast of the seated figure becomes the mouth of the profile head, a mouth open in utterance.[14] Both images—provocatively seated nude female and freely speaking woman—are apparent on the cover of Fumiko's text, connoting not only uninhibited self-presentation but also the obtrusive enunciation of that position by a female speaker. These twinned areas, female body and female mouth, which pictorially both nurture and define the other, present an intriguing configuration that gestures to the interconnection of body and language in the construction of the Hayashi female poetic subject.

Reading this graphic representation as body conjoined with/in speech/writing signifies a further conception of body, one that is culturally specific: that is, in Japan, mind and body are not conceived as separate entities. The mind/body 'split' and other binarisms characteristic of much of western thought are not traditional philosophical problems in Japan. In fact, Japanese conceptions of mind/body seem closer to the formulations of Maurice Merleau-Ponty, or of feminist thinkers, such as Elizabeth Grosz and others, who see the mind/body as interrelated and interdependent rather than divided. In this sense, the 'bodies' depicted on the cover of Fumiko's poetry collection take on ever more fully the sense of the whole person, mental, physical, cultural, sexual, and so on, than a cursory western reading might assume. This is not to deny, of course, that western representations and conceptualizations of the body were unknown in Japan at this time. On the contrary, imported western ideas of the body had been making their way into the country from the Meiji period and earlier, bringing new perspectives in art, literature, medicine, and anatomy among others. Although acceptance and assimilation of such ideas varied, any reading of Fumiko's body/bodies must take into consideration the intermingling of traditional/nativist ideas with those of the west. Perhaps one of the most important of these imports as regards Fumiko's body/text is the western preference for artistic representations of the nude female body, a cultural model firmly in place in the west by the nineteenth century[15] yet largely ignored in Japan (except for pornographic or erotic prints) until the advent of the Meiji period.[16] At the time in which Fumiko wrote, the female nude was a familiar if still exotic form of western-inspired artistic representation. Employed by Fumiko on the cover of her text in a way that attends to the erotic-discursive, the nude female body may be read further as disturbing traditional patriarchical-elitist notions of how women should be and act. That Fumiko's western/modernist design gestures to her poetry as a site of writing not only the body but the speaking/writing *female* body signals resistance to the dominant masculinist Confucian ideology with its resultant privileging of male over female.

Even though women have been writing in Japan for more than 1200 years and have left their mark as major innovators and trendsetters in the classical tradition, perceptions of women and of women writers have always been problematic. With the modernization of the country in 1868 and the subsequent re-structuring of Japanese society, problems of reading and writing women mushroomed as literary practice underwent significant change. While it is true that new opportunities for women arose, particularly in matters of education, the new order did not make it easier for women to write. On the contrary, most found themselves pressed into the "good wife, wise mother" (*ryōsai kenbo*) mold, a Meiji construct that, coupled with laws which excluded women from political activity, made it very difficult for women to seek empowerment through literary and/or socio-political discourse. Nonetheless, the "new women" of Meiji did not hesitate to venture onto literary paths. In many cases, the female body was put forward as textual site wherein female subjecthood could be conceptualized, explored, written, as for example, in the writings of Higuchi Ichiyō (1872-1896) and Yosano Akiko.

Due to the privileged place accorded women's writing in the classical Japanese literary canon, modern Japanese women writers were faced not so much with the difficulty of establishing female subject positions per se but rather with a need to inscribe literary undertakings with a 'modern' female subjectivity. Yosano Akiko, whose poetry early on attempted to bridge the gap between classical tradition and western-derived modernity, created a stunningly sensual aesthetic that celebrated the imaginary of a modern female self. Setting out the

R. Hayashi Fumiko's *I Saw a Pale Horse* (*Aouma wo mitari*). L. Yosano Akiko's *Tangled Hair* (*Midaregami*).

female 'self' as the basis of her writing, Akiko presented a new tantalizing vision for women poets and writers. In the Taishō period (1912-1925), new formulations of female subjecthood continued to appear despite government censorship and suppression. Rather than personal aesthetic, many writers, especially those connected with the magazine, *Seitō* (*Bluestocking*), focused on women's issues and related social problems. The female subject acquired dimension, and the female body became the site of social critique.

Fumiko, belonging to the 'third-generation' of modern Japanese women writers, began to write at a time when women of the lower social classes were entering the urban workforce in unprecedented numbers. Life in the city had become a possibility for young women who previously could look forward only to employment in the textile mills and spinning factories of newly industrialized Japan. Moreover, due to the persistence of feminists in the New Women's Association (*Shin fujin kyōkai*), laws banning women from political activity were lifted in 1922, with a resulting increase in participation by women in political movements. Women's writing also burgeoned, the 1920s being one of the most prolific periods for women writers this century. Poor and working-class Japanese women, emerging for the first time in Japanese history from centuries of silence, were now able to assess at firsthand the life of the Japanese 'mainstream.' Those who found voices, like Fumiko, began to speak and write, telling their own stories, bringing new subjects to textual 'life.'

Understandably, many of these new writing women selected auto-biographical modes as the means of self-speaking. Fumiko chose autobiographical prose *and* poetry as the means of articulating her presence. One of the reasons for Fumiko's poetic focus was the ease with which she could jot down her feelings and impressions at odd moments during the course of a working day, or while roving about from one place to another.[17] Fumiko's poetic practice is thus akin to that of American poet, Audre Lord, who observes that poetry can be an "economical"[18] means of self-writing for many women writers, given the constraints of their lives. Citing further the connection between poetry and autobiography in the writings of women poets as varied as Emily Dickinson and Adrienne Rich, Celeste Schenck also notes that "first-person poetry . . . in its supposition of personhood has provided women writers of lyric with infinitely more immediate access to subjectivity that the novel or other literary genres . . ."[19] Fumiko, too, in her assumption of female subjectivity chose to construct a living, breathing, working female body as the narrating figure of an immediate, lived experience.

The body as the site and/or "home" of autobiographical practice for contemporary women writers has been taken up by Sidonie Smith, who notes that "the body of the text, the body of the narrator, the body of the narratee, the cultural "body," and the body politic all merge in skins and skeins of meaning."[20] In this regard, Fumiko's textualization of "body," as read by Enchi and others, would seem to (re)present a similar plethora of "bodies," all of which determine and demarcate in a variety of ways the poetic-autobiographical subject of *I Saw a Pale Horse*. The historical and cultural "body" of Fumiko's text, for example, is that of late Taishō—early Shōwa Japan. All of the poems that appear in this collection as well as the poems selected from Fumiko's *Diary of a Vagabond* were written in this period. Spanning the years 1922 to 1928, Fumiko's poems straddle an era of considerable political and cultural change, encompassing the influx of Marxist ideology, the demise of anarchism, the Great Kantō Earthquake, and the appearance of the working urban woman. Nonetheless, Fumiko's poetic voice did not resound with the ringing tones of her Taishō foremothers, such as the founder of *Seitō*, Hiratsuka Raichō (1886-1971), who proclaimed her belief in 'woman as the sun,' nor did Fumiko evince the powerful yet genteel feminism of poets like Yosano Akiko or Fukao Sumako (1893-1974). Instead, Fumiko wrote as outsider, social outcast, tramp. A contentious and impertinent spirit moves her words, part of a new *zeitgeist* at work in the late Taishō era, one in which the working woman began to play a major role in the life of the nation. Accordingly, it seems fitting that by the time Fumiko had gathered her favourite poetic pieces together and published them in a single volume, the old era was no more and a new era—Shōwa—was well under way.

Fumiko's unconventional texts have been viewed by Miriam Silverberg as express representations of the *modan gaaru* or "Modern Girl" phenomenon of the 1920's. This scholar sees the promiscuous, nomadic life-style extolled in Fumiko's poetry as but one aspect of the new, multi-faceted urban women's culture that arose in Japan during this time.[21] In this context, Fumiko is viewed as typical of her times, the new adventurous 'working' woman as opposed to the intellectually awakened but as yet unemployed 'new woman' of Japanese feminism a decade earlier. While Fumiko may be read as illustrative of Modern Girl norms and behaviour, it is important to note that Fumiko was living in an eccentric manner, quite outside the strictures of ordinary Japanese society, long before the Modern Girls made their appearance. That she was able to integrate her early life within the Modern Girl phenomenon and give expression both to individual experience as well as to the experience of many other women was one of her great talents. Such written expression also brought Fumiko and her uncommon lifestyle before the public eye.

Thus, Fumiko's appeal to the Japanese reading public rests not only on the large body of historical and cultural evocations, such as the *modan gaaru*, associated with her work but also on the public perception of her life as "unconventional," hence, as a site of the exotic, a source of endless fascination to her biographers. Many facts of Fumiko's early life, however, remain unknown. Further, a great deal of Fumiko's early "biography" rests on details that are taken from her *own* early writings, such as *Diary of a Vagabond*, a text which is composed as much of "fiction" as "fact." Separating biographical data from fictional creation in the Fumiko life story has been the task of several scholars and yet, the Fumiko narrative continues to resist attempts at naturalization. In short, discrepancies or inconsistencies that have come to light seem to little affect the popularly perceived image of the Fumiko "body." So convincingly constructed, Fumiko's fictions have acquired legendary dimensions, and her life story as it appears in *Diary of a Vagabond* or in later texts, such as *One Life (Hitori no shōgai,* 1939), is accepted for the most part as 'true.' *I Saw a Pale Horse* belongs to these early life writings in which the female persona is read as autobiographical figure.[22] In fact, the female poetic subject of this collection is, along with the female subject of *Diary of a Vagabond*, the earliest of Fumiko's textually created selves.

Early Life: From Peddler to Poet

Keeping the above in mind, and also with the awareness that this is but one attempt to negotiate a path through the thorny thickets of the various narratives attached to the name Hayashi Fumiko, we may briefly set out some of the elements common to all these narratives and elucidate those which seem to have particular significance to the domain of lived personal experience that so permeates the corpus of Fumiko's early writing. Thus, biographical consensus places Fumiko's birth on 31 December 1903 in Moji near Shimonoseki in the extreme west of Japan.[23] The illegitimate daughter of itinerant peddlers, Miyata Asatarō (1882-1945) and Hayashi Kiku (1868-1954), Fumiko was never acknowledged by her natural father, Asatarō, with whom she lived until the age of seven. As a result, the stigma of illegitimacy was to follow Fumiko throughout her life. In Japan, where all births must be recorded in the family register, this is a fate from which there is no escape. Unacknowledged children like Fumiko are recorded in the mother's register in a manner which indicates the lack of paternal recognition. Since the facts recorded in the family register are reviewed upon entry into virtually every level and area of Japanese life, the mark of illegitimacy is a cruel one. Refused legitimate membership in a household, the illegitimate child, or *shiseiji*, is cast adrift, alone in the world, without prospect of social acceptance or family inheritance, the only surety being, as one researcher has it, "the loving relationship between the mother and child."[24]

The matrilineal has from early times played an important role in Japanese society. Not until modern times (that is, with the emergence of Japan as a modern state in 1868) did patriarchal values attempt to eclipse and/or replace ancient practice.[25] Thus, Japanese writing women and their relationship to the social body are in a somewhat different position from that of their western sisters whose experiences have been described variously as constituted by "absence," "lack," "nonessentiality" and so on in relation to western social and discursive practices.

In Fumiko's case, the exceedingly close matrilineal bond combined with the lack of conventional patrilineal social status were to create a disturbing tension. On one hand, as the result of her strong ties to the matrilineal, Fumiko possessed an unswerving self-confidence and yet, on the other hand, she functioned with an acute consciousness of lack owing to the virtual absence of patrilineal and/or patriarchal bonds, hence her overwhelming desire to be accepted by the status quo.

In many of her writings, both autobiographical essay and fiction, Fumiko condemned the father who had abandoned her. In "Talking About My Father" (*Chichi o kataru*, 1941), for example, Fumiko writes: "When I was a high school girl, there were times when I stuck pins in my father's photograph."[26] Yet as biographer Takemoto Chimakichi points out, Fumiko also wrote how "free" she felt not to be accorded status in her father's family register, and further, that being a *shiseiji* had never really bothered her at all. Takemoto speculates that such admissions as the latter as well as any acknowledgement that her father treated her kindly as a child would have brought down the entire Hayashi fictional construct.[27] This line of argument, which attempts to determine the "truth" of Fumiko's autobiographical female subject(s) by casting an "historical eye" upon biographical evidence and/or lack of evidence, is problematic at best. The fact remains that, whether "true" or not, Fumiko chose to present herself in the pages of her texts as a woman deprived, devalued, and dispossessed, and further, as a woman writing against patriarchal values. In *Diary of a Vagabond*, Fumiko gives vent to her feelings of lack and deprivation in a relentless, metaphorical downpour of emotion:

Somewhere someone was singing like rain falling in the street. Heavy rain. Disgusting rain. Anxious rain. Shapeless rain. Fanciful rain. Poor rain. Rain when no night stalls are set up. Rain in which one feels like hanging oneself. Rain in which one wants to drink *sake* because one is a woman. Rain in which one becomes excited. Rain in which one wants to make love. Rain like my mother. Rain like an illegitimate child. In the rain I simply walk aimlessly.[28]

The decision to focus on the self as *shiseiji* challenged social norms and discursive practice. By placing her female subject in a marginal area, Fumiko was able to institute her own discourse of resistance that introduced into the popular domain as personal story important issues long neglected and/or ignored by Japanese society at large.

Fumiko's attack on patriarchal narrative was further reinforced by her representation of an exceedingly close mother and daughter relationship. Hirabayashi Taiko, for example, describes the relationship between Hayashi and her mother, Kiku, as being as close as "Siamese twins."[29] Another point of connection between the two women was undoubtedly their mutual unofficial

12

status. For just as Fumiko remained unacknowledged as a child of her father, so Kiku never acquired the status of wife. That Asatarō, the eldest son of a farming family, seemed disinclined to exchange marriage vows with Kiku was due in part to Asatarō's position as eldest son. The great age difference between them, Kiku being some fourteen years older, as well as the fact that she had previously given birth to another child, not Asatarō's, also made her an unseemly candidate for the position of legal wife in the eyes of Asatarō's family. There were also rumours of other children born to Kiku. Asatarō, an astute business man, who in the seven years since Fumiko's birth, had parlayed his peddling business into a prosperous concern, seemed unperturbed by his domestic arrangements. He also brought a young geisha into the household. Soon after this, Kiku walked out, taking the young Fumiko, and Asatarō's chief clerk, with her.

Together with the former clerk, Sawai Kisaburō (1888-1933), a man even younger than Asatarō, and her mother, Fumiko began her seemingly endless peregrinations over most of western Japan. Interestingly enough, this foster father would also come in for his share of drubbing, portrayed as a weak and ineffective ne'er-do-well in the pages of Fumiko's later texts. Living for a time in Shimonoseki where her foster father opened a used-clothes store and, when the shop failed, with her maternal grandmother in Kagoshima, Fumiko gradually lost all sense of stability. Eventually her unlucky parents took to the road and Fumiko with them. Lodging in cheap inns, hawking low-quality goods along the roadside, occasionally attending school, Fumiko's movements are unclear until the family once again enters historical record in the town of Onomichi on the coast of the Inland Sea where Fumiko, by now thirteen years of age, enrolled in the local elementary school.

In Onomichi, Fumiko grew to adulthood, working part-time, attending school, writing poetry. In spite of the seemingly settled existence, however, the family frequently moved within the town of Onomichi, and Kisaburō continued peddling. The uncertainties of the roving life were never dispelled. As Fumiko was to write in *Diary of a Vagabond* about her early years, "Travel was my home."[30] Indeed, the town of Onomichi as well as the larger cities of Shimonoseki and Kagoshima all claim Fumiko as native daughter, underscoring the disjunctive nature of the center, the "native place," against which Hayashi constructs her poetic subject. Perceiving her position as one of lack, that is, of unrecognized child denied the identity of homeplace, Fumiko's poetry, more than that of other modern Japanese poets, cries out most plaintively for the security and comfort of "the old home," "the old village." Nostalgia functions as a reminder of the poet's chaotic past, the impossibility of claiming origins; hence, the need to fictionalize, and most importantly, the desire to construct identity.

The first step in the creation of a poetic/textual 'self' came with Fumiko's decision to leave Onomichi for Tokyo in 1922. There she would eventually come into contact with other writers and poets, women and men who were in the forefront of the literary movements of the day. Nonetheless, Fumiko was only nineteen, recently graduated from Onomichi Girls High School, and at first more inclined towards marriage than literature. Her intended fiancé, a student at a private Tokyo university, was the scion of an Onomichi area family. Having followed him to Tokyo to await his graduation, Fumiko undertook a variety of low-paying jobs to make ends meet. The marriage, however, never took place. Facing strong objections from his family who disapproved of Fumiko and her background, the young man broke with her and returned alone to Onomichi. This rejection excluded Fumiko still further from the ranks of conventional Japanese society. The failure of female desire, akin to the instability of home and family ties, would become yet another sensitive area in the construction of poetic subject.

Following on the heels of this personal shock came another violent upheaval, the Great Kantō Earthquake of September 1923, which drove Fumiko from the capital to her mother and foster father in Shikoku. The stay was a short one, however, and Fumiko returned to Tokyo early in 1924, bringing with her a diary, which she called "Utanikki," or poetic diary. In this diary she had begun to record her thoughts and feelings in a mixture of prose and poetry. This diary, which expanded over the next four years to at least six notebooks, provided the material for Fumiko's best-selling *Diary of a Vagabond*, and also for *I Saw a Pale Horse*.

Upon her return to Tokyo, Fumiko again moved from one job to another, working first as a maid for the writer, Chikamatsu Shūkō (1876-1944), and then as shop attendant, waitress, factory worker. She also entertained ideas of becoming an actress and managed to secure an introduction to modern theater actor and poet, Tanabe Wakao (1889-1966). This connection would prove to be a fruitful one for Fumiko. A mutual interest in poetry and theater quickly blossomed into romance, and Tanabe and Fumiko began sharing quarters. During the few short months the couple spent together, Fumiko, through Tanabe, made contact with modernist poetry circles. In spite of her lowly background, Fumiko did not find the new company at all daunting. One of the members of Tanabe's group later recalled:

> Tanabe thereupon introduced a young woman, who was sitting to one side, as his wife, saying she wrote poetry. If she had been an ordinary housewife, she would have made us tea and then retired, but when someone said, "What kind of poetry do you write? Please read us one of your works," she promptly stood up, went to fetch her manuscript, and then, without the least hesitation, recited one of her poems.[31]

As in this early instance, Fumiko's enthusiasm and desire for recognition frequently overrode social custom, a trait that would endear her to later feminist critics,[32] but in the context of the times brought gossip, criticism, and sometimes outright opprobrium.

14

Fumiko and Anarchist Poetry

The poets with whom Fumiko now began to keep company and who remarked on her lack of feminine reserve were by no means conformists, but like most male members of Japanese literary circles of those days, their revolutionary ideas did not encompass a feminist agenda. Including such men as Hagiwara Kyōjirō (1899-1938), Tsuji Jun (1884-1944), Takahashi Shinkichi (1901-1986), Okamoto Jun (1901-1978), and Tsuboi Shigeji (1897-1975), these poets were among the vanguard of modernist poetry in Taishō Japan. Associated with dadaism and anarchism, as well as with the new proletarian literature of the left, Fumiko's literary companions were themselves a motley group. Their gatherings, centered in the Nantendō, a French-style restaurant located on the second floor of a building in the Hongō section of Tokyo, included women as well as men. Here, Fumiko met Hirabayashi Taiko as well as Tsuboi Sakae (1899-1967) and other women writers and poets for the first time. In spite of the designation "anarchist," most of those who gathered at Nantendō were interested in literary themes and ideas and were not necessarily political activists.

Anarchism, one of the dominant socio-political theories of Taishō Japan, along with Marxism-Leninism, attracted large numbers of writers and poets in the 1920s, Fumiko no less than many others. In the early Taishō years, however, socialist and anarchist political movements often shared mutual concerns, a situation which continued for about a decade, creating a kind of ideological mix. Eventually, however, anarchism began to lose ground, suffering from the influx of new ideas kindled by the Russian Revolution. The movement was crippled still further when one of its most influential adherents, Ōsugi Sakae (1885-1923) and his female companion, the writer and former editor of *Seitō*, Itō Noe (1895-1923), were shot by military police in the aftermath of the Great Kantō Earthquake in September 1923. By the late 1920s, many members of the Nantendō group had shaken off their anarchist origins. Some, like Tsuboi Shigeji, joined the proletarian movement. Others moved onto different paths entirely, like Takahashi Shinkichi, who turned to Zen. Still others attempted to adhere to their anarchist beliefs until overtaken by death, obscurity, or the militarism of the 1930s. Nonetheless, at the time when Fumiko began to write, battle lines were still being drawn, and clear boundaries were not yet established. For this reason, Fumiko's poetry is viewed sometimes as "proletarian" and sometimes as "anarchistic." Fumiko, however, belonged fully to neither camp.

Anarcho-dadaist poetry, on the other hand, being less concerned with political theory than with revolution in poetic language, continued to thrive throughout the decade. Hagiwara Kyōjirō, for example, was a principal spokesman for anarchist poetry. In his lengthy *Death Sentence* (*Shikei senkoku*, 1925), Kyōjirō attempted to kill off what he deemed to be old and antiquated in modern Japanese poetry. An astonishing poetic array, aggregations of words, phrases, and alphabet letters erratically punctuated and arranged, *Death Sentence* gradually disintegrates into a bewildering conglomeration of signs and shapes, a true decimation of conventional poetic language. Kyōjirō, who experimented with freeing poetic expression from the stereotypes of the past, found a kindred spirit in Takahashi Shinkichi, another Nantendō poet intrigued by the absurdities of language. His collection, *Poems of Dadaist Shinkichi (Dadaisuto Shinkichi no shi*, 1923), edited by Tsuji Jun, the anarchist critic and former husband of Itō Noe, was already well-known by the time Fumiko made her appearance at Nantendō.

Besides Kyōjirō and Shinkichi, the poet Tsuboi Shigeji was also influential in anarchist literary circles. Tsuboi, for example, was instrumental in launching anarchist literary magazines, such as *Aka to kuro (The Red and the Black)* in 1923 and *Damu damu (DamDam)* in 1924. In the first issue of *Aka to kuro*, Tsuboi proclaimed: "Poetry is a bomb! Poets are the dirty criminals who will throw the bomb at the resisting walls and doors of prisons!"[33] Such diatribes became the norm for the magazine which went on to declare in a later issue: "Be negative! Be negative! Be negative! We shall devote all our energy to negativity!"[34] Not surprisingly, Tsuboi became known as a poet of "rebellious, intense, negative spirit."[35] Such an unrestrained poetic manifesto as Tsuboi's was to appear in Fumiko's poetry, too, yet without the revolutionary platform. Instead, Fumiko directed the scathing anarchist vision towards her own life, demolishing through her poems the prison wall of past personal experience. Rather than a new poetic language, from among her scattered poems a new poetic persona began to emerge. Giving voice to this new poetic "self" would become Fumiko's work over the next five years, resulting finally in her poetic assemblage, *I Saw a Pale Horse*.

Besides male poets, Fumiko also made the acquaintance of female poets who frequented the Nantendō. One of these women, Tomodani Shizue, was an actress and former protegé of the writer Tamura Toshiko (1884-1945). Also a friend of Tanabe Wakao, Shizue wrote surrealist poetry but was not herself an anarchist. Shizue joined Fumiko in her first poetic venture, the publication of a poetry pamphlet entitled *Futari (We Two)*. Securing the publication fees of twenty yen from one of the wealthier Nantendō poets, Kanbe Yuichi (1902-1954), Fumiko and Shizue brought out the first issue of their magazine in July 1924, sending copies to all the Nantendō regulars. Among these early poems by Fumiko were "Lord Buddha" and "Red Slipper," which later would be included in *I Saw a Pale Horse*. Although *Futari* lasted only three or four issues, this was the first major declaration by Fumiko of her poetic ambition. Having returned to Tokyo seven months earlier, Fumiko had spent her time well. She had made contact with poetry circles, found a place among a lively if indigent group of like-minded artists and, most importantly, established herself as a poet.

Thus, Fumiko gained much in her association with the anarchist poets. Not only did she make friends and alliances, she also absorbed their opinions and ideas, their theories of poetry, and their readings of foreign literatures. Nonetheless, Fumiko retained her own idiosyncratic stance, taking the measure of anarcho-dadaist discourse in ways which subvert its play with language, capping its irrationality with her own, as in the following passage from *Diary of a Vagabond*:

Dadaist poetry is popular. It's a poetry of childish tricks. Word games. Blood does not flow in it. It can't speak of desperate, honest matters. It's just reckless. Yet I think I'll close my eyes and try to write one of these. I'll write a poem about a parasol and a crow. When I close my eyes, associations suddenly pop up from the blackness. I think only of odd things. First, a memory of a smell. Then watery tears fill my nose. I scream mutely, as if I've been gobbled up by an alligator. My breasts are as heavy as four tons and I tip over like a bag of *udon* flour. A white star appears on my finger nail. I've heard that's a good omen, but I don't believe it.[36]

Here, Fumiko critiques the poetry of dadaism for its avoidance of the experiential. For Fumiko, poetry that is not inscribed with the 'flesh and blood' of the poet is nothing more than a series of futile exercises based on meaningless associations and abstractions.

Her descriptions of the anarchist poets themselves also focus on the immediately personal. Fumiko writes:

Takahashi Shinkichi is a good poet. Okamoto Jun, too, is a fine poet. Another surpassingly good poet is Tsuboi Shigeji. He wears a black Russian shirt and lives in lodgings so cramped and narrow eels could sleep there. Hagiwara Kyojirō is a passionate poet in the French style. He wears a jacket striped like a bumble-bee. What's more, all these poets are supremely poor, just like me.[37]

"Good poets" though they may be, we are not treated to examples of their work but to descriptions that betoken eccentricity and poverty, apparent requirements of a poetic lifestyle that Fumiko does not hesitate to appropriate for herself. Poetry, for Fumiko, seems to be as much a matter of the lived life as it is of language.

Through the anarchist poets, Fumiko also became familiar with works of anarchist ideologues, particularly the writings of Max Stirner (1806-1856). Today considered a precurser of Nietzsche, Stirner advocated a kind of psychological anarchy in which human beings were exhorted to "Realize yourself!"[38] This call for the primacy of the ego no doubt struck a chord in Taishō intellectuals in their pursuit of personal freedom. Facing innumerable obstacles, both social and political, in their quest for autonomy, many writers, especially male writers of the *bundan*, or literary establishment, early shied away from active confrontation with the Japanese state. Favouring the *shi-shōsetsu*, a form of writing that privileged personal experience over all else, such writers turned to their personal life for literary inspiration. Stirner's catch-phrase fit well with the Taishō emphasis on the personal, ignoring as it did the realities of social and political restraints. For many Taishō writers, the pursuit of inner freedom seemed a safer path to follow than the road to political or social emancipation.

Critiques of Stirner, particularly those of Marxist orientation, centered on the observation that the call for self-realization lacked any comprehensive social dimension, leading to the conclusion that Stirner's egoistic dictum was "realizable (only) by individualists such as artists."[39] Indeed, the Japanese anarchist poets, in their concern with language and poetic expression, formed a defiant and articulate avante-garde, yet one unable to effect social change. In the case of Fumiko, the 'self-centered' anarchist credo gave impetus to the portrayal of the female vagabond, victim and outcast, struggling to realize her own inner, dynamic potential in spite of the forces arrayed against her.

Although Fumiko, like the Taishō anarchists, could not fail to respond to the call for personal liberation, her outlook, as that of many women of the time, was tempered by an acute awareness of social injustice. Women writers of *shi-shōsetsu*, for example, were more likely to describe a personal world impinged upon by outside factors: strikes, the low status of women, the hardships of the working poor, the danger of political activity being but some of the areas explored in these writers' texts. Social and political reality was never at a far remove from the site of writing.[40] The tendency of women's texts to engage wider issues was a phenomenon of early Taishō and continued to derive considerable momentum from "left-wing" writing that began to appear in Japan around 1921-1922. Among the more successful advocates of this new proletarian writing were female writers, such as Miyamoto Yuriko and Sata Ineko. That women of this period were at the forefront of new literary production is a fact often overlooked by Japanese scholars, yet nonetheless the leading female figures of modern Japanese literature were establishing themselves at this time.

Following her debut in *Futari*, Fumiko, with the help of her Nantendō associates, continued to publish her poetry in various magazines and newspapers, including left-wing publications like *Bungei sensen* and the anarchist periodical, *Mavo*. One of these early *Bungei sensen* poems, "Song of a Female Factory Worker" (*Jokō no utaeru*, 1924), borrowed the polemical appeal as well as the imagery of poverty and destitution employed by other proletarian writers and poets:

> Although I am poor
> I think of flying up into the sky —
> I — my legs are anchored

with iron chains!
In jail
my view is obstructed!
— through a small window —
the trembling of one green leaf
teaches me the breadth of the great sky.
Don't make a fool of me!
I believe in my strength.
Even though I am poor, I am strong.
I am not sad.
Because of this poverty,
because of my solitary strength,
like a worm slowly crawling
for the sake of x x x, day after day
I live in torment.
Between my clamped lips
my back teeth
strike out sparks
in unbearable vexation
and are gradually worn down.[41]

Despite the lack of ideological formulation, Fumiko's female factory worker succeeds in conveying the corporeal resistance of the female worker to her existence. The worker's refusal in the poem to succumb to seemingly hopeless circumstances was also a feature observable in Fumiko's own efforts to become a published poet. Unflagging in her determination, Fumiko made the rounds of other poets and writers, showing them her poetry and asking for help in securing publication. According to Fumiko, Tokuda Shūsei (1872-1943), the well-known naturalist writer, was so moved when he read her poetry that he immediately lent her money.[42] By August 1924 Fumiko had left Tanabe and moved in with a young proletarian poet, Nomura Kichiya (1903- ?). Nomura, already successful in publishing poetry in a variety of magazines, brought out his first poetry collection in October of that year. Known for his sorrowful depictions of abject poverty, Nomura was, in fact, living much as he described. To a great extent, Nomura's poetry was concerned with not having enough to eat, as the following poem, "From the Darkness" (Yūyami kara), shows:

Suddenly the light came on
my head is spinning
from below I can hear the sound of evening rice bowls
unable to stand it, I look out the window
in all the houses even the one opposite
        people are eating dinner at large tables

Staggering, faltering, I go out
From all the houses light leaks out blissfully
happy voices flow forth
and in every house alike they're heading for their meal.

I alone am left out in the cold
I alone have not eaten for three days
Everywhere without exception is the sound of happy rice bowls.[43]

Written during the time he and Fumiko were living together, Nomura's exceedingly prosaic language and self-pitying resignation provide a telling contrast with Fumiko's plucky female factory worker or with other colorful poems by Fumiko on hunger and poverty, such as "I Want To Say How Senseless It All Is" (*I Saw a Pale Horse*) and "Fly To Me, Boiled Egg!" (*Diary of a Vagabond*). In order to support Nomura and herself while they wrote, Fumiko continued working as a cafe waitress and in a variety of other jobs. The constant strain of little money and near starvation proved to be too much for the frail Nomura, who vented his anger and frustration on Fumiko. After suffering repeated beatings, Fumiko moved out, no longer able to stand the physical and emotional abuse meted out by her partner. The liaison with Nomura had lasted off and on for nearly two years.

To leave or to stay, to give up or to try again, like many women enduring the tirades of an abusive husband, Fumiko was plagued by indecision. Registering feelings of guilt, pain, anger, and regret, Fumiko attempted to assuage her distress through writing. The six poems that deal with the Nomura relationship in *I Saw a Pale Horse* are written from the standpoint of a woman who has left "that man" behind. Compared to *Diary of a Vagabond* or to other later prose works, such as "A Record of Honest Poverty" (*Seihin no sho*, 1931), where the Nomura relationship is dealt with at length, the poetry collection condenses the episode. Nomura is simply not "there"; he is promptly dismissed from the text as the female persona takes precedence, empowered by her solo status.

In life, however, in spite of the disappointment with Nomura, Fumiko did not remain long alone. By December of 1926, she was preparing to marry the man who would be her life companion, Tezuka Ryokubin (1902-1987), a western-style painter. In January 1927, the couple settled into a new life together. Poor but happy, Fumiko wrote and Tezuka painted backdrops for the stage. For the next year and a half Fumiko published little. Together the two travelled to Onomichi, to Nagano to visit Tezuka's family, and to Shizuoka where Fumiko's parents were living. It was a good match; Tezuka encouraged Fumiko in her writing, proving a constant and steady support. At long last, Fumiko's chaotic personal life had taken a turn for the better.

I Saw a Pale Horse: A Poetic Autobiography

Fumiko's literary career was also about to receive a much-needed boost. In July 1928, playwright and novelist, Hasegawa Shigure (1879-1941), launched a new magazine, *Nyonin geijutsu* (*Women's Art*), to provide a forum for women writers, poets, and critics. Shigure's magazine helped establish a literary reputation not only for Fumiko but also for many other Japanese women writers.[44] Without the opportunity provided by *Nyonin geijutsu*, a number of female literary careers would have been much longer in the making, and some might never have materialized at all. Shigure, having achieved success herself as a writer, was aided in her venture by her husband, Mikami Otokichi (1891-1944), a keen admirer of Hayashi's poetry. With Mikami's recommendation, Fumiko's poem *Mugibatake* ("Millet Field") was printed in the August issue of *Nyonin geijutsu*. This poem would later become the introductory *Jijo* ("Preface") of *I Saw a Pale Horse*. Fumiko also submitted a selection from her poetic diary, *Aki ga kitan'da*, ("Autumn has come"), which was brought out in the October issue. Subtitled *"Hōrōki"* (literally, A Record of Wandering; or, in my translation, *Diary of a Vagabond*), a name suggested by Mikami, the diary was an instant success. In all, over the next two years, twenty installments of Fumiko's *Diary of a Vagabond* would appear in *Nyonin geijutsu*.

Fumiko's *Diary of a Vagabond* was an unparalleled success, selling 600,000 copies when it appeared in book form in 1930 and catapulting Fumiko to the heights of literary fame and fortune where she reigned until her sudden death from overwork in 1951. A vivid, rambling account of Fumiko's own down-and-out existence amidst the cafes and bars of 1920s Tokyo, *Diary of a Vagabond* not only gave voice and recognition to a new female underclass, it also established a new female subject position in Japanese letters, that of the intrepid 'picara,' keen to explore her alterity as working and writing woman, and as poet.

Although a number of Fumiko's poems were incorporated into the prose text of *Diary of a Vagabond* (reminiscent of Japanese poetic diary format), Fumiko was not satisfied. She desired to be read first and foremost as a poet. Determined to bring out her own poetry collection, Fumiko sought the aid of her friend, Matsushita Fumiko, who agreed to put up the fifty yen necessary for publication. As a result, in June 1929, *I Saw a Pale Horse* made its appearance, long overdue perhaps in terms of Fumiko's poetic accomplishment but still well timed as regards the poet's capacity to recognize and to set in order what she had so far achieved.

Thus, the poetic subject of *I Saw a Pale Horse* is constructed according to a realized poetic vision, one which has been edited and shaped over time. Tōmaru Tatsu notes that *Diary of a Vagabond* and *I Saw a Pale Horse* share eight of the same poems, yet there are differences in diction and wording, the poems in the poetry collection being superior.[45] Mori Eiichi goes further to show

how certain of these poems have been reworked by the poet from the time of their first publication until acquiring their final form in *I Saw a Pale Horse*.[46] Moreover, the ordering of the collection does not follow the chronology of writing, poems being arranged according to the poet's choice. This deliberate revising, selection, and conscious ordering of contents without regard for publication history would seem to point to some intent on the part of the poet.

Since Fumiko makes only the briefest comment on her compilation of *I Saw a Pale Horse*—"I gathered together only those poems I liked best among those (I wrote during) the past ten years"[47]—we have little indication of the poet's intent in making the arrangement. Nonetheless, even a cursory reading of the collection reveals, for example, great disparity in tone and mood between the first poem and the last. This fact alone has caused one Japanese critic to read the entire collection as a "spiritual journey" from misery to happiness.[48] If this is the case, then might we not expect to find further evidence of transformation within the collection as a whole? Or more specifically, can the collection be read as a progression that moves from an initial problematic declaration to a final harmonious resolution?

The concept of poetic progression is ancient in Japan—early poetry anthologies were arranged according to certain 'rules' of association and progression while the composition of linked verse in the medieval period was also undertaken with regard to such subtleties. An examination of the Fumiko text, however, shows that, in general, classical forms and conventions are not in evidence, with one possible exception: the suggestion of a *johakyū* movement. That is, the first eight poems (from "Preface" to "Heavy Heart") act as an introductory section, the next twenty poems (from "Buying Sea Bream" to "Red Slipper") provide amplification and modification, and the last six poems (from "Red Sails Gone to Sea" to "Flowers on a Moonlit Night") a smooth, quick finish.[49] This type of dynamic can be found not only in linked poetry but also in various forms of Japanese music and drama,[50] leading to the conclusion that Fumiko's arrangement of poems, while perhaps not able to claim actual semblance with earlier practice, is nonetheless suggestive given Fumiko's interest in theater and other traditional, popular performance arts, an interest that continued throughout her life, traces of which can be observed not only in her poetry but in her essays and *shōsetsu*.

Diary of a Vagabond and I *Saw a Pale Horse* are closely linked as poetic texts, as autobiograhical debut writings, as works with common thematic elements, and in the case of eight poems, as writings that possess a shared textuality. The *Diary*, however, by virtue of length and the inclusion of prose text, is a grander undertaking, one that writes a vivid and varied panorama, scene after scene multiplying dizzily into a whirl of images, a truly modernist montage. By contrast, the poetry collection is reduced, compact, a distillation of the diary into poetic form. Culled from a profusion of texts, *I Saw a Pale Horse* represents the poet's attempt to impose order upon, and construct meaning from, the events and experiences of her own life, and perhaps even the sprawling text of *Diary of a Vagabond*. Both writings, in spite of their difference, are implicated in the formation of the Fumiko subject, the Fumiko narrative, to the extent that a discussion or presentation of one without the other would be tantamount to erasing part of the Fumiko construct. Thus, the poetry collection *I Saw a Pale Horse*, offered here in its entirety in translation, is accompanied by a selection of translated poems from *Diary of a Vagabond*, poems that reveal further the diversity and ingenuity of Fumiko's early oeuvre, and expand and complement the reading of *I Saw a Pale Horse*. In order that Fumiko's poetic voice may speak first, commentary on the poems will follow the translations.

Notes

1. There are other statues commemorating Hayashi Fumiko in Japan, in particular on Sakurajima in southern Kyushu, the maternal family home, where a charming, barefoot statue of the young Fumiko can be found. I am indebted to Carl Yokota of Richmond, British Columbia for this information as well as for some delightful photographs of this site.

2. The inscription is a quotation from *Diary of a Vagabond* (*Hōrōki*, 1928-1930). See *Hōrōki* in *Hayashi Fumiko zenshū*, vol. 1 (Tokyo: Bunsendō, 1977), p. 394.

3. Hayashi Fumiko, *Hayashi Fumiko zenshishū*, ed. Itagaki Naoko (Tokyo: Kanna shobō, 1966), p. 247.

4. An early call for a new look at *I Saw a Pale Horse* came from Odagiri Hideo, "Sakuhin kaisetsu," *Nihon gendai bungaku zenshū: Hayashi Fumiko, Hirabayashi Taiko*, vol. 78 (Tokyo: Kodansha, 1967), p. 419. Recent studies include Tōmaru Tatsu, "Umoreta shijin no shōzō" *Gendai shi bunko: Hayashi Fumiko shishū*, No. 1026 (Tokyo: Shichōsha, 1984) and Mori Eiichi, *Hayashi Fumiko no keisei—sono sei to hyōgen* (Tokyo: Yūseido, 1992), the latter devotes one chapter to *I Saw a Pale Horse*.

5. Mori, p.39.

6. Tōmaru, p. 144.

7. Modern poetry histories (with focus on *shi*, or free verse, and excluding traditional poetic forms, such as *tanka* and *haiku*), outlines of modern Japanese literature as well as collected works of Shōwa literature put out by major Japanese publishers

seldom treat the works of early Shōwa women poets writing in the *shi* form. Tōmaru Tatsu points out that selections from *I Saw a Pale Horse* appear in only two such collections: *Nihon gendaishi taikei*, published by Kawade shobō shinsha, 1951, and *Nihon shijin zenshū*, published by Sōgen bunko, 1952 (Tōmaru, p. 144).

8. Those who make mention of this story include Hirabayashi Taiko; her husband Kobori Jinji; Tsuboi Sakae; Takahashi Shinkichi; and Tsuji Jun.

9. Tōmaru, p. 145.

10. Tōmaru, p. 146.

11. Ueda (Enchi) Fumiko, " 'Aouma wo mitari' hyō," in *Nyonin geijutsu*, vol. 2, no. 8, 1929, p. 112. Enchi wrote at this time under her birth name. Interestingly, the preface by Tsuji Jun to *I Saw a Pale Horse* makes a very similar point: "Above all, I feel you (Fumiko) are not a "counterfeit" poet. You write poetry with your entire body." See Tsuji Jun, "Jo" *Aouma wo mitari*, (1929; rpt. Tokyo: Nihon kindai bungakkan, 1981), p. 4.

12. Hirabayashi Taiko, "Sehyō to kanojo - Hayashi Fumiko no tame ni," in *Nyonin geijutsu*, vol. 2, no. 9, p. 66.

13. Tōmaru, p. 142.

14. Such reverse figures or patterns were subjects of study by psychologists of the times. One well-known pattern was that of "Rubin's wineglass" (*Rubin no sakazuki*) or "Rubin's chalice" (*Rubin no tsubo*) after Edgar John Rubin (1886-1951) in which two human faces in profile also describe the shape of a wineglass or chalice.

15. Peter Brooks, *Body Work: Objects of Desire in Modern Narrative* (Cambridge: Harvard University Press, 1993), p. 16. See also Chapters 4 and 5 for further discussion of this phenomenon in western art and narrative literature.

16. In his book *Reflections of Reality in Japanese Art* (Cleveland: Cleveland Museum of Art, 1983), Sherman E. Lee points out that representations of pornographic nudes in Japanese art were often stylized to the point of indecipherability, "verg(ing) on caricature, even the surreal." See p. 187 and note 9, p. 207. Clearly, representations of the female nude in traditional Japanese art are based on a very different set of aesthetic concerns and priorities from that of the west.

17. Hayashi Fumiko, "Ketteiban 'Hōrōki' hashigaki" in *Hayashi Fumiko zenshū*, vol. 16 (Tokyo: Bunsendō, 1977), p. 218.

18. Quoted by Celeste Schenck, "All of a Piece: Women's Poetry and Autobiography" in *Life/Lines: Theorizing Women's Autobiography*. (Ithaca: Cornell University Press, 1988), p. 292, note 36. Schenck refers to Audre Lord's "Poetry Is Not a Luxury" in *Sister Outsider: Essays and Speeches* (Trumansburg, N.Y.: Crossing Press, 1984), p. 36.

19. Schenck, p. 292.

20. Sidonie Smith, *Subjectivity, Identity, and the Body: Women's Autobiographical Practices in the Twentieth Century*, (Bloomington and Indianapolis: Indiana University Press, 1993), p. 128.

21. Miriam Silverberg, "The Modern Girl as Militant," in *Recreating Japanese Women, 1600—1945*, ed. Gail Bernstein (Berkeley: University of California Press, 1991), p. 253.

22. The conflation of author/narrating persona as a common strategy of discourse in Japanese literature, elsewhere studied in the works of male writers, is also to be found in the writings of Japanese women, such as Hayashi Fumiko. (See Edward Fowler, *The Rhetoric of Confession*, for a thorough discussion of this phenomenon in the works of male *shishōsetsu* writers.)

23. The actual birth may have been earlier in the year, perhaps in the spring or early summer. This is the season commonly cited by Fumiko in her autobiographical writings that mention her own birth, and is also vouched for by her mother. Such a discrepancy may have resulted from Kiku delaying registration of the birth until the last possible moment, hoping for Asatarō's recognition of the child. See Takemoto Chimakichi, *Ningen: Hayashi Fumiko* (Tokyo: Chikuma shobō, 1985), pp. 14-16. This kind of disparity is typical of information on Fumiko's early life.

24. Shimazu Yoshiko, "Unmarried Mothers and Their Children in Japan," *U.S.-Japan Women's Journal*, English Supplement, No. 6 (1994), p. 103.

25. As Karatani Kōjin observes: " . . . until very recently Japanese society maintained a matrilineal structure (although strictly speaking we should call it bilinear, in the sense that matrilineal and patrilineal structures co-existed)." Karatani Kōjin, *Origins of Modern Japanese Literature*, tr. and ed. Brett de Bary (Durham and London: Duke University Press, 1993), p. 169. For more detailed discussions of this issue, see Sharon H. Nolte and Sally Ann Hastings, "The Meiji State's Policy Towards Women, 1890-1910" and Kathleen S. Uno, "Women and Changes in the Household Division of Labor" in *Recreating Japanese Women 1600-1945*, ed. Gail Bernstein (Berkeley: University of California Press, 1991).

25

26. Hayashi Fumiko, "Chichi o kataru" in *Hayashi Fumiko zenshū*, vol. 16 (Tokyo: Bunsendō, 1977), p. 140.

27. Takemoto Chimakichi, *Ningen: Hayashi Fumiko*, (Tokyo: Chikuma shobō, 1985), pp. 28-29.

28. Hayashi Fumiko, *Hōrōki in Hayashi Fumiko zenshū*, vol. 1 (Tokyo: Bunsendō, 1977), pp. 462-463.

29. Hirabayashi Taiko, *Hayashi Fumiko*, (Tokyo: Shinchōsha, 1969), p. 3.

30. Hayashi Fumiko, *Hōrōki in Hayashi Fumiko zenshū*, vol. 2 (Tokyo: Shinchōsha, 1951), p. 5.

31. Tsuboi Shigeji, "Mumei jidai no Hayashi Fumiko," *Gendai shi bunko: Hayashi Fumiko shishū*, p. 135.

32. Tanaka Yukiko in *To Live and To Write: Selections by Japanese Women Writers 1913-1938* (Seattle: Seal Press, 1987) describes Fumiko as "a dedicated and hard-working artist, and one of the few women writers of her day who dealt aggressively with male publishers and editors and used her popularity to her own advantage." (p.103).

33. Hayakawa Masayuki, "Tsuboi Shigeji," *Kindai shi gendai shi hikkei* (Tokyo: Gakutosha, 1989), p. 9. A detailed discussion of the male anarchist poets is presented by Hirata Hosea in his chapter "Modernist Poetry in Japan" in *The Poetry and Poetics of Nishiwaki Junzaburo: Modernism in Translation* (Princeton, New Jersey: Princeton University Press, 1993), pp. 131-148.

34. Itō Shinkichi, "Aka to kuro," *Nihon kindai bungaku daijiten*, vol. 5 (Tokyo: Kodansha, 1977), p. 6.

35. Hayakawa, p. 69.

36. Hayashi, *Hōrōki in Hayashi Fumiko zenshū*, vol. 1 (Tokyo: Bunsendō, 1977), p. 469. *Udon* flour is a wheat flour used to make noodles.

37. Hayashi, *Hōrōki in Hayashi Fumiko zenshū*, vol. 1 (Tokyo: Bunsendō, 1977), p. 470.

38. John Carroll, *Max Stirner: The Ego and His Own* (London: Jonathan Cape, 1971), p. 32.

39. John Carroll, *Break-Out from the Crystal Palace: The anarcho-psychological critique: Stirner, Nietzsche, Dostoevsky* (London: Routledge and Kegan Paul, 1974), p. 85.

40. Janice Brown, "Reconstructing the Female Subject: Japanese Women Writers and the *Shishōsetsu*," *B.C. Asian Review*, Winter 1993-1994, pp. 23-24.

41. Adachi Ken'ichi, ed. *Gendai nihon bungaku arubamu 13: Hayashi Fumiko* (Tokyo: Gakushū kenkyūsha, 1974), p. 133.

42. Hayashi Fumiko, "Bungakuteki jijoden," in *Hayashi Fumiko zenshū*, vol. 10, (Tokyo: Bunsendō, 1977), p. 4.

43. From Nomura's second collection, *The Three-Cornered Sun* (*Sankakukei no taiyō*, 1926) in *Nihon gendai shi taikei*, vol. 8 (Tokyo: Kawade shobō, 1951), pp. 209-210. Although Nomura disappears from the pages of Shōwa literary history in later years, and his fate remains unknown, Nomura and Fumiko continued to be associated in one poetry history, their photographs appearing side by side as late as 1951. See *Nihon gendaishi taikei*, vol. 8, frontispiece.

44. Some of the writers who benefited from publication in *Nyonin geijutsu* include: Enchi Fumiko, Yagi Akiko (1896-1983), Matsuda Tokiko (1905-), Nakamoto Takako (1903-), Yokota Fumiko (1909-1985) and others. For a full treatment of women writers and *Nyonin geijutsu*, see two works by Ogata Akiko: *Nyonin geijutsu no sekai* (Tokyo: Domesu shuppan, 1980) and *Nyonin geijutsu no hitobito* (Tokyo: Domesu shuppan, 1981).

45. Tōmaru, p. 158. The eight poems are: "Lord Buddha," "Song in Distress," "The Queen's Homecoming," "Taking Out the Liver," "Lone Journey," "Woman Dead Drunk," "My Ship Has Sailed," and "Red Slipper."

46. Mori, p. 23.

47. Hayashi Fumiko, "'Aouma o mitari' kōki," in *Hayashi Fumiko zenshū*, vol. 16. (Tokyo: Bunsendō), 1977), p. 197.

48. Referring to the arrangement of poems, Mori Eiichi views *I Saw a Pale Horse* as an attempt to "trace the spiritual journey of one woman" (Mori, p. 36). Reading the collection as a progression inspired by the poet's own self-searching, Mori observes the shift from the lonely and confused female figure of the first poem, "Preface" (*Jijo*), to the calm and wondering female "I" of the final poem, "Flower on a Moonlit Night" (*Tsukiyo no hana*). Yet the manner in which this transformation is accomplished is not clearly accounted for. Mori postulates that "Preface" is the frame of the collection, evoking an "inescapable reality" which the poet longs to flee.

Most other poems fit this frame. Those that do not are so-called nostalgia poems, longing for the old home, parents, and so on. The second poem in the collection, the title poem, is one of these. Nostalgia poems are interspersed with poems of inescapable reality, providing a "spiritual stabilizer" (Mori, p. 34) for the poet's misery. The final poem has a "different character from all that has gone before" (Mori, p. 35) and presents a changed persona, one that is happy and settled in self and in relationship. The manner in which poems of inescapable reality and those of nostalgia are interspersed, leading to the calm atmosphere of the final poem, however, is not detailed. This analysis, which posits a kind of see-saw dialectic leading somehow or other to a final resolution, is suggestive, and represents a rare critical attempt to examine the text in detail. In my opinion, *I Saw a Pale Horse* does exhibit a marked thematic progression, but an exceedingly more complex one than Mori's interpretation would allow.

49. According to Konishi Jin'ichi, *johakyū* is a kind of poetic "principle" which distinguishes structure as well as "tempo or pace of progression;" it provides less a conscious framework than a "hidden order," particularly as it occurs in renga, or linked verse. See Konishi Jin'ichi, "The Art of Renga" in *Journal of Japanese Studies*, vol. 2, no. 1, Autumn 1975, pp. 49-50. In the case of Fumiko's collection, *johakyū* might thus be viewed as a kind of substructural element, 'hidden' or suggested but not necessarily consciously installed by the poet.

50. *Gagaku, nō, joruri,* and *nagauta* exhibit *johakyū* format. See William P. Malm, *Japanese Music and Musical Instruments* (Charles Tuttle: Tokyo, 1990).

Part II

Poems

I Saw a Pale Horse

33

Preface

Ah, the pain in this twenty-five-year-old woman's heart!

The twenty-five-year-old woman stands in a millet field
where the color of the sea barely shines
the corn! the corn!
how much it pains her breast
the twenty-five-year-old woman
gazes blankly at the sea.

One, two, three, four
the little grains of corn are the sadly wishful babble
of the twenty-five-year-old woman
the breeze from the blue sea
the breeze from the yellow field
the sighing of the black earth
dampens the heart of the twenty-five-year-old woman.

In the coastland millet field
what sort of hopes rage
over the murmuring hard leaves?
The twenty-five-year-old woman
truly wants to end her life
she truly wants to die.

Stretching up, stretching up
one pitiful ear of corn
has made it this far.
The twenty-five-year-old woman
truly does not need a man
a sadly difficult toy
when she grows tired of a real household
shall she live or shall she die?
Anyway, she has sorrowfully resigned herself

she longs for real friends
each with an honest heart—
all the millet leaves are restless
desperately
in her heart the twenty-five-year-old woman
wants to throw everything away and run off
close one eye
open one eye
ah, there's no way
she wants a man and she longs to travel.

Shall she do this
shall she do that
tediously pulling thread from a ball of yarn
tired of living so pointlessly
the twenty-five-year-old woman
lies down on the path in the millet field
and wishes she could fall into a deep sleep.

Ah, just such
helpless confusion
in this twenty-five-year-old woman's heart.

I Saw a Pale Horse

I Saw a Pale Horse

The barn in my village is far away.

On a moonlit night when all the cherry blossoms had bloomed
I was the one who ran to the harbour
with my red *Diary of a Vagabond* in the hazy moonlight
winding my white muffler around my neck
it was I who loved steamships
yet . . .
in the window of the police cell, my arm hurting
I see the pale horse of my distant village
"Father!
"Mother!
"Take care of yourselves!" I call out.

In the midst of a scene I have begun to forget
walking dejectedly
one pale horse!
ah, it has begun to disappear a little now
from my field of vision
pale horse!

The barn in my old village is far away
and now
father's face
mother's face
appear clearly
in the scene of my old home
the ones who loved me
were my old parents barely eking out a living
and in the dilapidated barn
the old pale horse.

All you dizzying noises, go away!
Shall I ride the pale horse,
threading my way through the trees around that deserted
house?!
In the midst of this abundant nostalgia
stupid! stupid! stupid!
in the window of the police cell
I smell the distant barn.

Red Ball

I am a red ball thrown out in a field!
when a strong wind blows
high into the wide sky
I fly up like an eagle!

Storm wind, strike!
filling the burning sky
storm wind, quickly
strike me, the red ball.

Under the Lantern

If you give me ten cups of King of Kings[1] to drink
I shall throw you a kiss
ah, what a pitiful waitress I am.

Outside the blue window, rain falls like drops of cut glass
under the light of the lantern
all has turned to wine.

Is Revolution the wind blowing north . . .?
I've spilled the wine
opening my red mouth over the spill on the table
I belch fire.

Shall I dance in my blue apron?
"Golden Wedding," or "Caravan"
tonight's dance music . . .

Still three more cups to go
How'm I doing? you ask
I'm just fine
although I'm a nice girl
a really nice girl
I scatter my feelings
generously like cut flowers
among petty pigs of men.
Ah, is Revolution the wind blowing north . . .?

Lord Buddha

I've fallen in love with Lord Buddha[2]
when I kiss his cool lips
ah, I'm so undeserving
my heart is benumbed.

So unworthy am I
from head to toe
my calm blood flows against its tide
seated on the lotus
so composed and graceful
his manly bearing
bewitches my soul.

O Lord Buddha
how can you treat me so coldly!
O Lord Buddha
you won't persuade me to chant
your cold-hearted prayers
my heart is like a broken bee's nest
with your manly bearing
leap into my flaming breast
stained by earthly life
is this woman
embrace her unto death.

O blessed Lord Buddha.

Returning Home

Gazing at the mountain and the sea of my native village,
  I weep
after a long absence I've returned to my old village home
the child I played house with long ago
the child who was my "husband"
is now a young man like a great tree
putting barrel hoops on a large bath tub
the sound of his hammering fills the small village.

The person with whom I linked little fingers on the rough
  wooden bridge
has gone to an unknown country, they say.

Shall I call out "Hey!"
as I gaze out to sea from the top of the small hill where
  the tangerines grow?
The people of the village, my friends of the village
will probably all come with an answering shout.

Lament

Neighbors
relatives
lovers
what are they to me?

If that which I eat in life is not satisfying
then the pretty flowers I have painted will wither away
though I want to work cheerfully
I squat so pathetically small
amidst all kinds of curses.

I try to raise both arms high
but will they all betray such a pretty woman?
I cannot always hug dolls and keep silent.

Even if I am hungry
or without work
I must not shout Wo-o!
lest the fortunate ones knit their brows.

Although I spit blood and die in agony
the earth certainly won't stop in its tracks
they are preparing healthy bullets one after another
in the show window
there is freshly baked bread
ah, how lightly beautiful like the sound of a piano
is the world I've never known.

Then all at once
I feel like crying out: goddammit![3]

Heavy Heart

That night—
above the table in the cafe
a face like a vase full of flowers
even if a crow caws on some tree
I won't care.

Night is cruel—
filling both my hands
my face
tired in shiny powder
pulling the hands of the clock to twelve.

Buying Sea Bream

Buying Sea Bream

—for Tai-san[4]

A kind of excitement might be a medicine for us.

The two of us like kindergarten children
walked together through the town's nooks and crannies,
        our legs moving in unison
the woman who shares my fate
exchanged glances with me, looking into each other's eyes
        we smiled sadly
damn it!
laugh! laugh! laugh!
if only two women laugh
modesty is useless in this hard world.
In order not to lose out to the people of the town
let's send a year-end present to the country.
Sea bream would be good
its sweet taste is agreeable
my native place on the coast of distant Shikoku
there
my father lives
and my mother lives
and the house, the hedge, the well, the trees . . .

Isn't that right, young fellow!
Send something with a large advertisement on it labelled
        Edo-Nihonbashi[5]
father and mother who have little pleasure
will go about with such happiness, bragging to distant
        neighborhoods
—Our daughter has bought this and sent it to us from
        Edo-Nihonbashi
here, have some
oh, thank you . . .

This woman
her home deep in the mountains of Shinshū
her brown cape swelling out
uttered a cry, her teeth always white.
—tomorrow's wind will blow tomorrow, so let's buy
         something with all the money and send it off . . .
in the young shop boy's wooden box are fried fish meal,
         salmon sprinkled with sesame, sea bream dried in
         sweet sake

Sensing the same laughter, the two of us
stood at Nihonbashi.

Nihonbashi! Nihonbashi!
Nihonbashi is a good place
white gulls were flying past.

The two of us walked somehow sadly, holding hands
let's break through that hard-as-glass sky
singing a song from *The Lower Depths*,[6] the two of us
         laughed
as if bursting out of that restless city.

I Want To Say How Senseless It All Is

—to my parents at home

I want to say how senseless it all is, one thousand times, ten
thousand times
I want to shout how senseless it all is, one thousand times, ten
thousand times
somehow or other . . .

Even so, we are three cheerful people—parents and child
but counting the days to buy one cup of rice
is no way to live.

It's not that we've lived carelessly
but like a work horse who from morn till night
props up its four legs
frantically
because it wants to eat
we've simply ended up living like that!

If parents and child together
at least shout how senseless it all is
one thousand times, ten thousand times
one thousand times, ten thousand times
maybe we will be happy.

Sobering Up

Dear world!
I'm drunk now.

The wall of the lodging house is pale like a rice cracker
in my purse is thirty *sen*.

It's raining so I'll bring my wooden clogs inside
the person who got me drunk
said to love him without making any conditions
and I did
but I'm sad . . .

Tomorrow night I'm going to the matrimonial agency
and look for a man—

The fee for my lodgings is thirty-five *yen*
ah, it seems I'll become a mad woman
even if I work hard for a month
my husband is as slippery as a sea cucumber.

I wish I could kiss someone, just like smoking a cigarette
I don't need a lover

For just one whole month
I want to eat white rice in peace
my mother has rheumatism
and I am near-sighted
wine is bad for my head—
I was sending fifty *sen* at a time to my mother
but now I've split up with that man
my head swims
fifty *sen* and thirty-five *yen*!
I guess it all won't fall from heaven.

Love is in the Heart

What distant memories does a young virgin have . . .
knowing all about men
a frog swims in this filthy vein.

There is a field so wide
but you say you can make flowers of truth bloom
          anywhere
capricious young women are always looking at airplanes
even if a million women and men meet and yet not one is
          sincere
the battle of the sexes will take a holiday.

Turkeys and badgers![7]
What is this! Away with you, world!
Those women and men who cannot scatter the spark of
          true love
split them right down the middle with a bang!

The Queen's Homecoming

It's farewell to that man!
In my chest children wave red flags
have I made them all that happy?
without going anywhere
I shall live, waving red flags with them all.

Everyone run out for me!
And carry stones
and toss me on your shoulders
put me on top of a stone castle.

I won't cry over this farewell!
I'll keep my spirits up, keep them up
wave a flag for me
the poverty-stricken queen has come home.

Taking Out the Liver

In the chicken liver fireworks scatter, and night comes
ladies and gentlemen! hear ye, hear ye!
the final scene with that man has come slowly but surely
in his bowels
sliced open with one sword cut
a killfish swims smartly.

It's a fetid, stinking night
if no one is home, I'll break in like a burglar!
I'm poor
and so that man has run away from me
it's a night that wraps me up in darkness.

Lone Journey

There's a wind-howling white sky
a splendidly cold winter sea
even a crazy man whirling in a dance would waken to
        sanity
in such a great ocean
I'm on the direct route to Shikoku.

Blankets twenty *sen*, sweets ten *sen*
third class cabin like a pot for half-dead loaches
a terrible seething

Spray
spray like rain
gazing out at the wide sky
I grip my purse with eleven *sen*.

Ah, I'd like to smoke a cigarette
but even if I yell "Wo!"
the wind will carry my voice away
in the white sky
the face of the man who has made me drink vinegar
is so big, so big

Ah, it's really lonely travelling alone.

Good Demon, Bad Demon

Well, anyway, I shall celebrate this chance meeting with
        you
—Isn't it a lonely life
being truly alive?

Sometimes I even think it's an illusion
and so it may be
but these days, separated entirely from sexual desire
my heart wants to make love
as if it were a locomotive.

Sexual anarchy and
virtuous communism stink, don't they?

Of course, even in my heart
there are good demons

—I'm surprised
just as bad demons make me dance naked
so do good demons make me proud of myself.

Wait!
I'm now going to invent a remedy for life and death
it's something I've always thought about
I want a machine that can walk
taking steps on the wide sea
—So, let's talk leisurely
we're still alive, aren't we . . .
we both have another twenty or thirty years.
Meeting you so unexpectedly by chance
on this small globe
is just as it should be
even if we don't mention karma.

When I think of all the optimistic views of life people
      have
there are so many -isms I can't count them
all of them a battle between good demons and bad
      demons.

Finally, the sky is wide
how would you like to smoke a Green Bat[8]
from this six-*sen* packet
laugh happily
and celebrate today's chance meeting?

Dwarf in the Ashes

Today the sun has already set
in the faint white gloom
as I was staring at the ashes in the brazier
on top of the uneven surface
a dwarf came stepping along
carrying a bag like a poppy seed.

—There's nothing to worry about, lady
poor people are lucky, he said, heh, heh.
Ah, I was tired
and so sad I began to cry
when my large teardrops fell into the ashes
the dwarf vanished with a sizzle and a puff.

Heart of Autumn

An autumn sky!
trees, air, water
coldly clear like the mountain's skin.

Veiled in mist like a woman
the night sky is unbearably fine
by day
or by night
autumn is fine.

In the blue medicine bottle
the light of the red lantern
flickering, flickering
the lovers who pass through the town
waving their walking sticks
I shall put into an old match box
and like a young girl
wind them round and round with yellow cotton thread.

When I see the dawn colors of the nearby forest and
              hear the sounds of the birds
my heart seems to break into crimson
walking along late night country roads
I hear the insects' voices
and my broken love turns to salty tears
blown by the wind

Autumn is fine
both day and night
my life stretches on like a rail.

Kiss

The night I first kissed
the cherries were blooming under the lanterns

the moon was red—

his lips, which seemed as if they would suck blood
even when parting
even when parting
on his lips the moon danced round and round.

Words of a Romantic

—Take that and give up!
—Not yet, not yet . . .
—Now, with this you'll give up!
—Not yet, not yet . . .

The god of poverty was roaring and striking my
    shoulders
so I laughed and wrote in large letters on the
    pawnshop gate:
"Weak ones, your name is woman."

A Clear View

"Gone to sea!" the mouth of the department store seems
    to shout
spitting to one side
kicking me as if I were a small pebble
hoisting their mismatched, out-of-date flags
a throng of miserable people pass by.

When I am pushed by the noise of the town wrapped in
    twilight
I think of white rice in the suburbs.

Recalling those bright, healthy houses
I played the flute high in the sky, I loved the sound of
    copper coins
But I know I'm a hen that hatches only faulty eggs
and I end up crying.

So I'll put those small dirty eggs into a cloth bag
and there, at the mouth of the department store
I'll throw it at the heads of the crowd.

Like the wind I turn the merry-go-round
and blow sweetly on suburban flower gardens.

The pleasures of honest living
are not to tell lies and to eat white rice every day
"So Fumiko is lucky!"
Just once I want to shout that to someone.

Dear Katyusha

Dear Katyusha

1

The sunflower has grown right up.

It's a hot, sultry August!
How many times I went through that tunnel
carrying a grey cloth bundle on my back
In those days
in Nōgata, a town like the bottom of a kettle,
the lovely song "Katyusha"[9] was popular
coal miners and the women who pushed the trolleys
all loved that sweet song.

2

I was strong like a hard onion
behind the mountain range where the moon rose
"at least before the snow melts . . ." went the song
from the coal mine to the town was a distance of almost
        one mile.

Day after day I patiently set out ten-*sen* white fans with
        paintings of carp and Mount Fuji
and sold them
when I passed the blue-painted company living quarters
        that looked like a ship-wreck
the miner's dirty tenements were lined up like green caterpillars
all the miners' wives were waiting for me.

3

When lunch time came
the gong resounded throughout the coal mine
as if eagerly waiting
people poured from the earth like pebbles
"Hey, Katyusha! Bring us our food!"
even on the rough ground, sunflowers bloomed
the miners gulped deep breaths of fresh air
and filled their mouths with food
they pinched their wives' noses
and tossed out lively laughter
It's a hot, sultry August!

4

The town of Nōgata is as lonely as a sea slug.
When I finish eating and go out to buy kerosene
the night breeze, set free,
skims across the jellyfish moon.
At the brothels where the miners go
the lanterns are whitely bright like seashells.

My step-father and my mother
passed through the town and the village
again and again

Pulling our cart we went out peddling
to the pottery works and the clog factory.

When I stood on the road, tired of waiting,
I could see the lantern of the cart, its load lessened,
        pulled along by my step-father
I ran like a dog
and clung to my mother who was pushing the cart.

5

The rain continued to fall day after day
on the second floor of our sweltering lodging house
how both parents and child would have loved a
    permanent dwelling.
When I went out to the town
I saw a signboard of a pretty foreign girl tapping on a
    train window
at a railroad station where snow was falling
in my notebook of those days
every page was full of Katyusha's face.

6

"Today we're going to smash the company office."
On a certain day
when I went to the coal mine playing, playing my flute
the windows of the miners' rooms which once were so
    quiet
were now in a tumult
and the empty trolleys floated like bobbins on the rails.

When I passed through the tunnel carrying my heavy
    bag on my back
the miners, strips of cloth tied round their heads, said,
"Hey! Katyusha, better go home; it's dangerous around
    here!"
I was a twelve-year-old girl
the fact that they called me Katyusha
made me happier than if the had called me princess
"Hey, fellows, don't give up!" I called back.

7

I did not overlook the pure smiles
from the faces of the free, cheerful miners
directed straightforwardly towards an innocent young
    girl.

When I returned to our lodging house
I parted my hair and gave myself Katyusha's hairstyle.
Dear Katyusha!

Katyusha, the serf girl, ended up miserably.
There were snowstorms, Siberia, prison, vodka,
    Nekhlyudov
but I was a poor girl who knew nothing
holding onto vast hopes
I grew up
like a vegetable box onion.

The Town Where One Can't See the Sea

The echo in the frozen sky
is the sound of a solid gong
when winter comes to roadside trees
the human stomach aches
worn out
worn out
the robots who throng together in the hell of the city
the platinum chain that links the robots' legs
is an electric current unrestrained by cost.

Imagine a day when the sound of the waves destroys the
            rough cement city that has no past and no future!
Break up marble and domes and build a tunnel
build a happy tunnel that runs to the sea
the sea, the waves
frothy as a new stage play
shake your hips, square your shoulders
puff out your chest
confess the painful truth to the sky.

The destruction of the polluted earth
is not comforting
Shall we strip off the large, cold roof
and sprinkle foam on the waves!
Or shall we squeeze a centipede
like glutinous jelly into the long, dark tunnel
while it holds the key to the chain!

You unfortunate electric dolls who throng together in hell
look at the wings of the flying eagle tapping the waves
Sea! Sea!
The sea is filled with light, free sailing ships.

Sweetheart

I jumped from the ship
in a straight line—
when I tried to right myself
a sea cucumber crawled along my calf
I felt shy
and I held my breasts with both hands.

When the waves become rough
I loosen my hair
already I've abandoned myself to despair
if we collide with a bang
our passion will rebound with a bang
ah, I love a kiss
that strikes me like a strong wave.

On a blue, velvety wave
I let my naked body be soaked in spray
simply amazed I'm drowned in the wave.

So, I'm a mermaid
hold me close,
my new lover.
My dreams are of a cute sailor
whom I've left behind on the ship
but my message to the white gull is:
"*You've* got a nice sweetheart."

Ah, I'm a miserable sort of mermaid
sea gull, you've flown away so far, so far
come back, hee-ro! hee-ro!
—I'm still so lonely
—I'm so lonely
—The blue mermaid is dead.

Passion for Snow

In the field a vast snowstorm
I become simply a single eagle
wings spread to the full
full of spirit
spreading out my passion as far as I can
One stroke!
I'll zoom over the field.

Twisting and turning
A beautiful cannonball of snow
I put on a red hat
both hands open wide
my heart opens wide
I open my eyes as wide as I can
rolling over and over I'll cover myself in snow.

That pure blueish-white snow!
Scattered clouds rising up from the snow
ah, rising up bit by bit my head a sphinx
I'll drink up the field, the mountains, the snow, the
        houses.

The sphinx on the snow
has breathed in the sky, tears flying from its eyes
mouth full
a full deep breath
rolling and shaking its breast as hard as it can.

On the glorious blossoming earth
cannon balls of snow fly gloriously
with all my strength
stamping my feet as much as I can
I shall draw the bow with all my strength!

Woman Dead Drunk

When rusted leaves like scraps of iron come fluttering
      down
and trees by the roadside stand like a forest of masts
then day after day comes the song of the wind.

Girl in the purple kimono coat and black boa!
That coat and shawl make me feel warm.
Beautiful woman
beautiful town
I must be strange
even though I work and work, I can't eat
and look at all those beautiful autumn clothes—

Your full, proud cheeks
have had enough to eat
between you and I how many hundreds of miles are
      there, I wonder—

I'm bored and I steal men
and so I drown myself in wine
people, all of them
throw me to the ground
and stamp all over me.
Young girl!
You're making yourself more and more beautiful.

Ah, this lonely dead-drunk woman
if she doesn't cry tears of blood, she'll go mad
even if she wants to shout
from inside a gramaphone
she stops herself, embarrassed in the moonlit night.

You weak, scornful women and men!
Carrying the casket of this dead drunk woman
under the town's forest of masts
with a happy song *su-to-ton, su-to-ton*[10]
I'll let you enjoy yourselves.

My Ship Has Sailed

On this muddy road
I stand like a broken-down car
this time I'm going to get myself into service and get
        some money
I want everyone to rejoice
didn't I arrive in Tokyo this morning from so far away
        after so many days?

I looked everywhere but there was no one to take me in
he said if he saw a movie and ate a bowl of rice and eels
        for fifty *sen* then he wouldn't mind dying
this morning I remembered that man's words
and I shed many tears

That man is at a lodging house
if I were there, the rent would go up
I walk about from cafe to cafe
sniffing aromas like a pig
love, relatives, society, husband
in my addled brain
I feel far removed from them.

I haven't the courage to want to shout
even if I want to die, I haven't the strength
hanging around my skirt, playing,
left behind in Shikoku
how are you now, kitten . . .
at the decorated window of the watch shop
I thought I'd try to look like a female thief
people only seeming to be human beings are swarming
        about

they say consumption will get better if one drinks soup
          made from horse droppings
making that cruel, cruel man drink that,
what sort of thing is lovers' suicide anyway . . .

Yes, yes, it's money
money, money, they say
but even though I've worked and worked, nothing comes
          to me
and they say money makes the world go round.

Don't miracles happen?
Can't something be done somehow?
Where does all the money I make disappear to?
And so finally I become a hard-hearted
worthless woman

Until I die I'll be a cafe waitress, maid, factory girl
worthless woman
I'll have to die working!

That sick, jealous man
said I was a red pig
arrows, bullets, fly to me
in front of these disgusting men and women
I want to show you Fumiko's bowels.

Red Slipper

I sit on this swivel chair that's the earth
and when it goes round with a thump
the red slipper I drag along
flies off.

So lonely . . .
even when I call "Hey!"
no one picks up my slipper
choosing courage, I throw myself from the swivel chair
shall I pick up the fallen slipper?
My cowardly hand still clings to the swivel chair.
Hey, anyone will do,
slap my face as hard as you can
and knock off my other slipper, too
I want to sleep for awhile.

Red Sails Gone To Sea

Red Sails Gone to Sea

Have you heard the sound of the tide?!
Have you heard the sound of the vast, wide sea?!

Entrusting the sooty lamps to their wives
the island factory workers kick pebbles along the beach
and gather on the sunset shore.

Have you heard the sound of the distant tide?!
Have you heard the voices of thousands of swarming
            human beings?!
This is a peaceful shipbuilding port on the Inland Sea
the narrow rows of houses on this island of Innoshima
            are
like the closed lids of seashells
trousers stained with oil and flags made of overalls are
            spread out
the sound of the factory gate being battered by brute
            force
that sound, wham, wham,
resounds over the whole island.

Whoooosh!
when the blue-painted service door is pushed by crowds
            of shoulders
the agile chameleons
holding account books colored with the blood and grease
            of the factory workers
jump nimbly into the launch
like foxes on a snowy night

From the factory workers' hardened faces twisted by
      emotion
tears of anquish gush
plop, plop, isn't that sound of their tears?
the fleeing launch
as it cuts in front of boats spread out like nets
then
the space between the fleeing launch and the workers
      thronging this small island
disappears in a single line of spray.

Even if they grit their teeth and rub their foreheads
      against the earth
the sky—
yesterday, today, too, it doesn't change
ordinary clouds stream past
Here!
The workers who have become crazy men, who have lost
      their heads
call the waves and howl at the sea
amidst the broken ships at the dock
they turn in a vortex and become an avalanche.

Have you heard the sound of the tide?!
Have you heard the sound of the distant waves?!
Wave the flags!

The vigorous young men
expose their shining skin
the cables whirring
straining with all their might at the ropes of the torn sails
they crash through the harbour gate
red sails set for the wind-howling sea!

Hey! Wave the flags!
Sing a song!
Though frayed and ragged
the red sails fill sturdily in the wind
kicking out white spray, they head to the sea!
Running like arrows to the middle of the ocean.

But . . .
hey, hey
calling out from the top of Storm God Mountain where the
          wind blows cold
prick up your ears at the shouts vigorous as the waves!
Poor wives and children
stand there on tiptoe
aren't they calling loudly to the sky, the sky!

Have you heard the sound of the distant tide?!
Have you heard the roar of the waves?!

Under the withered tree on the mountain
wives and children wave their hands together with the
          tree while deep in their eyes
the red sails are reflected forever
speeding along like sparks of fire.

Quiet Heart

It's late at night
in the distance the cock is crowing
tomorrow I shall buy rice with this
a fine children's story I have written
at my mandarin orange box desk
if I can get some money for it
my daydreams will vanish in the pure white electric light
        that illuminates the night.

Tired out, I try to bend my fingers
since I haven't eaten for two days
I'm very cold
look, my stomach echoes
like a bell, bong, bong.
I'll set a pot on the brazier
and make a heap of noodles to eat
outside the wind seems cold
a wonderful moonlit night.

When I look at the white thread of steam
I'm as happy as a baby.
I've finished writing the children's story
and I've boiled up the noodles . . .

The narcissus I planted a week ago has withered
it foolishly arouses my sad heart
and when I think of tomorrow I firmly choke back my
        tears
and look at my white hands.

Ah, long ago there was a person who wrote me love
        letters . . .

Burn!

Burn!
Burn!
This fire, these sparks.

Burn up my melancholy!
The sincere heart is a spark, a spirit!
Don't make a fool of me
don't ever make a fool of me
even if I'm poor
I'm alive!

Alighting atop a large tree
my child-like heart
really—it wants to shout excitedly
       like a mad person

Chain of Sparks

The morning when the radish field was white and frozen
washing the rice
I wished I had a red shawl
if I put on that red shawl
in the lightly, silently falling snow
and went on a trip with my lover . . .

My face turns red and I wrap up the trembling of my
           heart
tenderly my eyes swim with tears.

As I lean over the rice this morning my fantasies
stack up dream toys on an express train
burning like a chain of sparks
as it runs along.

Dream While Unemployed

In the burning dark night
the moon passes through a tunnel
in the offing a white sail
skips tirelessly along.
I was made to quit my job at the soap factory
my hands, roughened by caustic soda, look like caramel
I dipped them into perfume and wept.

How far I have walked I don't know
but anyway I can see a fire in the dark
I'm suitably hungry
and there's a Chinese restaurant
I was served a heap of fresh pork roast
One dish eight *sen*
I had warm thoughts
for the Chinese cook with shining eyes
on his arm touching mine
he entwined a snake, heh, heh . . .
when he brushed his hair out of his face
it was my cute boyfriend.
The trick snake jumped down!
Blue foam turned into hard soap.
My lover and I rolled over and over in the field, little
        fingers linked we came together and kissed
but because in this world he can't make enough to eat
he tried to shoot through my small breast
red sparks have turned to hard soap
I want to eat Chinese food
fleeing on the surface of the sea as fast as I could
bang! I lost my virginity.

Flowers on a Moonlit Night

"On the way home from visiting a prostitute
on a snowy lane
I saw a fox running," he said.
The painter was kicking like a child at the frozen road.

Walking in the suburbs
we went to buy red flowers
not for some years was there such a miracle of the heart
       as this
"Tomorrow shall I draw a still life of those flowers?" he
       asked
shaking his cape in the wind
as if he intends to hang it on the moon
I saw a fox running along a snowy lane

It was running and twisting its body like a wave.
The scene of that mountain brothel floated up before
       me and I thought sadly of myself:
       I'm like a kitchen vegetable box
when I recalled the pale white flower that bloomed
       inside that closed box, I cried.
"But . . . say!" he said,
"It's the scent of sweet daphne."
From the dark mansion
comes the faint lonely scent of the flower.

I held the red flowers up to the moon.
With a popping sound the flowers bought by the poor
       painter open in the moonlight.
No snow is falling
no fox passes by
on this bright moonlit country road in the suburbs.

Notes

1. A brand of whisky.

2. A translation of part of this poem appears as "The Lord Buddha" in *Women Poets of Japan*, tr. and ed. by Kenneth Rexroth and Ikuko Atsumi (New York: New Directions, 1977), p. 89. To the best of my knowledge, only two other poems from *I Saw a Pale Horse* have appeared in English translations other than my own. These are "Lament" (*Kurushii uta*), translated as "Song in Despair" by Ichirō Kono and Rikutarō Fukuda in *An Anthology of Modern Japanese Poetry* (Tokyo: Kenkyūsha, 1957), pp. 23-24, and "Returning Home" (*Kikyō*), translated as "Homecoming" by Hisakazu Kaneko in *Orient/West*, vol. 8, no. 1, May-June 1963, p. 48. Two poems translated by myself, "Under the Lantern" (*Rantan no kage*) and an excerpt from "I Want To Say How Senseless It All Is" (*Baka o iitai*), first appeared in "Hayashi Fumiko: Voice from the Margin" in *Japan Quarterly* (January-March 1996): p. 90; p. 95 respectively. The title of this poem, "Lord Buddha," is in Japanese, *Oshaka-sama*, a term of address that refers to Sakyamuni, the historical Buddha. In the final lines of her poem, which I have translated as "O blessed Lord Buddha!", Fumiko calls upon "Namu amida butsu no/ oshaka-sama!" Literally, "Sakyamuni, in the name of Amida Buddha!"—a mixing of the historical Sakyamuni with Amida Buddha, the central figure of worship in the Jōdo, or Pure Land, sect of Buddhism. Such confusion seems not uncommon. Kawabata Yasunari (1898-1972) mentions a similar "mistake" by Yosano Akiko in her poem on the Great Buddha at Kamakura in his novel, *The Sound of the Mountain*. Akiko refers to the Great Buddha as Sakyamuni, although the figure is actually Amida. See Kawabata Yasunari, *Yama no oto* in *Shōwa bungaku zenshū*, vol. 5 (Tokyo: Shōgakkan, 1986), p. 214.

3. In this poem as well as in many of her poems, Fumiko mixes informal and formal verb endings, a significant feature of her poetry in the original Japanese but one that defies translation. Fumiko thus may speak to the reader from diverse subject positions within the frame of the same poem. By shifting her style of speech, the poet subtly and sometimes abruptly alters the nature of the relationship between the "I" and the reader, a practice which can also emphasize her female voice, given the fact that women tend to use more formal speech patterns than men. According to Mori, such usage gives Fumiko's poetry "greater effect" (Mori, pp. 24-25). I am also indebted to Professor Sumie Jones for her perceptive observations on this poem at a conference on Women in Modern Japan held at the International Research Center for Japanese Studies, Kyoto, 9 March 1996. Professor Jones noted a variety of self-presentations, including the motherly, the confessional, the self as object of discourse and so on in Fumiko's poetic text. In general, then, we might say that Fumiko's mix of speech styles marks her poetic discourse as exceedingly complex, accompanied at all times by a contrasting and conmingling sense of both the humble and the defiant.

4. Hirabayashi Taiko (1905-1971), Fumiko's friend and confidante during the early years in Tokyo, was called "Tai." Sea bream is also "tai" in Japanese. Taiko's birthplace was in Shinsū (Nagano prefecture) as the poet later mentions.

5. Edo is the old name for Tokyo; Nihonbashi is the name of a bridge in the Chūō-ku section of the city and also the name of the area nearby.

6. A play by Maxim Gorki (1868-1936). Written in 1902 and translated into Japanese soon after, it was a popular favorite of the *shingeki* (new drama) stage.

7. The word for "turkey" in Japanese is literally "bird with seven faces" (*shichimenchō*). The badger, or *tanuki*, is a trickster figure. The poet is implying that certain men and women are fickle, changeable, and unreliable, like these animal figures.

8. A brand of cheap cigarette.

9. The heroine of *Resurrection*, a novel by Leo Tolstoy, popularized as a stage play in Japan during the Taishō era. See Part Three, note 5.

10. A Japanese popular song from around 1924. These syllables have no meaning. The song began: "If you hate going along with a *su-to-ton, su-to-ton*, then you're cruel."

Diary of a Vagabond

SELECTED POEMS

In This World Everything is Just a Lie

In this world everything is just a lie
over my head runs the last train bound for Koshū
I'm throwing away my life which is as lonely as a rooftop
        above a market
and spreading out my veins in the futon of a cheap inn.
I tried to hold onto that corpse pulverized by the train as
        if it were someone else
when I open the *shōji*, blackened by the dark night
even in such as a place as this, I find the sky, and the moon
        joking about

Goodbye to you all!
I've become a warped die, and so again I'll roll back over
here in this cheap attic room
gripping all the loneliness I've accumulated on this
        journey
I'm blown about aimlessly in the wind.

Spread Out In the Sky the Cherry Tree Branches

Spread out in the sky the cherry tree branches
lightly stained blood-red
there! from the tips of the branches pink threads dangle
passion's lottery

Unable to make enough to eat, the dancing girl threw
        herself into vaudeville
and danced naked, even so
that's not the fault of the cherry blossoms.

One single emotion
brings double obligation
amidst the cherries gloriously blooming in the blue sky
strange threads reel in
the naked lips
of every
living woman.

Poor, young girls
at night
I've heard them throw their lips
into the heavens like fruit.

The rose-pink cherries coloring the blue sky
are the fated kisses of these lovely women
the traces of lips turned aside.

Stubborn, Strong

Stubborn, strong
my poverty, my drinking, my pleasures
all those.
Ah, ah, ah

Slash them
knock them aside, send them flying
the things I've bewailed so many times, painful,
belching out art like spitting blood I shall dance and be
        happy like one mad.

On a Hill a Lone Pine

On the hill a lone pine
and below the pine
patiently looking at the sky am I.

Against the sky the needles of the old pine
shine like pins
ah, how indescribably difficult it is to live
how difficult to get food to eat.

There at my breast
I put my poor sleeves together
and with that old childish feeling
from the days when I lived in my old village
I beat on the trunk of the old pine.

I've Seen Fuji

I've seen Fuji
I've seen Mount Fuji
there was no red snow[1]
so I need not praise Fuji as a fine mountain.

I'm not going to lose out to such a mountain
many times I've thought that,
seeing its reflection in the train window,
the heart of this peaked mountain
threatens my broken life
and looks down coldly on my eyes.

I've seen Fuji,
I've seen Mount Fuji
Birds!
Fly across that mountain from dome to peak
with your crimson mouths, give a scornful laugh
Wind!
Fuji is a great sorrowful palace of snow,
blow and rage
Mount Fuji is the symbol of Japan
it's a sphinx
a thick, dream-like nostalgia
a great, sorrowful palace of snow where demons live.

Look at Fuji,
Look at Mount Fuji
in your form painted by Hokusai
I have seen your youthful spark.

But now you're an old broken-down grave mound
always you turn your glaring eyes to the sky
why do you flee into the murky snow?

Birds, wind
rap on Mount Fuji's shoulder
so bright and still
it's not a silver citadel
it's a great, sorrowful palace of snow that hides
                misfortune.

Mount Fuji!
Here stands a lone woman who does not lower her head
                to you
here is a woman laughing scornfully at you.

Mount Fuji, Fuji
your passion like rustling fire
howls and roars
until you knock her stubborn head down
I shall wait, happily whistling.

The Stars Are Blowing Trumpets

The stars are blowing trumpets
if you stab them, their blood will boil over
on a white bench thrown out like a broken shoe
looking like a prostitute
I gaze at the coldness of the countless stars.
In the morning
won't those shining stars disappear?
Anyone will do!
That woman on the white bench, she has scorned ideas
          and philosophies
please shower her with foul-smelling kisses
then this one reality
will satisfy her for awhile.

Birds Shine

Birds shine
even above the city they shine
the town filled with pollen   the tops of the telephone poles
tremble   they tremble
no place to stop
my lungs sing   a short colorful song.

In the brown rain
I walk holding my ears
My ears hurt   they hurt
the birds in the rain shine
struggling they fly
a dream of the wind over a bright field
my lungs sing   a short colorful song.

Where am I walking?
It's the birds' destiny
I was born somewhere or other, like the birds,
nights with nowhere to stay
shining they fly
but I don't shine
the surrounding rays of light burst out laughing
my lungs sing   only that . . .

A cat living alone   a dog living alone
just stones on a road where no one passes
the dew will vanish
a sky of birds   shining birds
shining smoothly like pulling out a nail
beckoning, beckoning   only shining birds
only my lungs are singing   that's all, just singing.

Bone of Fishbone

Bone of fishbone
grasses along the shore washed in the water's current
bone of fishbone
ashes floating where the bracken-colored clouds break
hello! comes the greeting from the river bottom
the Chinese character for agony   the Chinese
            character for woman
agony in the thighs
in thighs fragrant with slender beauty
the character for agony.

Bone of fishbone
drawing back the bowstring, offering with one stroke of
            the pen
bone of fishbone
again my love has been sent back
the Chinese character for sorrow   that character
everyone talks of it
in their bowels
a ship sinks in a sea of grief.

Complete self-forgetfulness!

In This City Different Kinds of People Congregate

In this city different kinds of people congregate
people corrupted by starvation
withered faces   a swirl of sick bodies
a low-class rubbish heap
it seems the Emperor is insane[2]
Tokyo, the diseased!

A still more terrible wind blows
ah, from where does that wind blow?
love affairs flourish   mildew thrives
there are no beautiful thoughts
nor fine ideas
living in fear
everyone is somehow terrified.

A pale angel appears from a crevice
Strange infinity . . .
in some mysterious fashion, the Emperor has become
          insane, they say
a pot of pantheists and enfeebled conduct
people congregating in a steady stream
groups of people guilty of something
the big clock of a city has begun to go crazy.

Fly To Me, Boiled Egg

Fly to me, boiled egg.
Fly to me, bean jam bun.
Fly to me, strawberry jam bread.
Fly to me, Chinese noodle soup.

A Raw Wind Blows

A raw wind blows
green shoots sprout
the road where dawn is breaking
shines the color of kerosene
a hushed morning in May.

Many dreams go up in smoke
skulls laugh
prisoners and officials, lovers, too
fellow travellers to the gates of hell
attacking each other is fine
nature decides people's lives
say! isn't that so?

I Came Home After Buying Ink

I came home after buying ink
I want to meet you somehow.
I want money.
Just ten-*yen* would be all right.
I want to buy a copy of *Manon Lescaut*[3], a *yukata*[4], and
       wooden clogs.
I want to eat my fill of Chinese noodles.
I want to go and hear *Sukeroku*[5] at Kaminari-mon.
I want to meet you just once.
Really, I want money.

I Beg Your Pardon, Sir

I beg your pardon, sir, but I'd like to say that
I am simply a woman who breathes
I know only of fifty *sen*, not a million *yen*
rice with beef costs ten *sen*
leeks and dog meat, isn't it
I'm like a small tumbling doll
a hothead who cries easily.

No, it's okay
any man will do
only to hold and sleep with
as I place a fifteen-*sen* cup of wine
on a saucer
absurdly carefree I deceive the world
being drunk feels great
I want to sing legions.

Where has it gone?
Is my hometown done for?
Nestling under the grape trellis
nestling
munching a piece of unripe fruit
I shall talk to you from morning till evening
from morning till evening . . .

Early Evening Light

Early evening light   I sleep quietly on evening islands
at the bottom of the sea throngs of fish
murmuring softly in elegant voices
whisperings of fish, jealousy of fish.
From a distant place the setting sun appears
above the earth, heralding the single paper layer of night
human beings moan in their sleep
evening islands   evening light

Soldiers leave their villages
students return to their homes
in their lives people moan
murmuring, it's my problem, too
is there peace in this world?
it's the feeling of hard, sticky sweets
what is human life, I wonder . . .
the torture continues
human beings sharing the torment.
Sooner or later these islands will disappear
only cows and chickens will survive
these two animals will interbreed
cows will grow feathers
and cockscombs
birds will grow horns
and cowtails.
Is there such a thing as eternity?
Eternity is the wind blowing beside your ear
evening light   islands merely floating
shaking like a baby carriage
archaeologists, too, perish in the end . . .

Winter Is Almost Here

Winter is almost here
the sky has said so
winter is almost here
the mountain trees say so.
The drizzling rain runs to tell us
the postman has put on his round hat.

The night has come to tell us
winter is almost here
the mouse has come to tell us
in the ceiling it has begun to make its nest.
Carrying winter on their backs
many people are coming from the country.

The Horse Wore An Ornamental Hairpin

The horse wore an ornamental hairpin
a horse pulling a load, staggering along
sweating buckets
a horse merely pulled along by fate

A horse pulled along by reins
sometimes blowing out white breath
there's no one to watch over it
sometimes with tremendous force it urinates
a whip strikes its buttocks
the pack horse climbing the hill

Where in the world is it walking to?
senselessly walking
no use in thinking at all.

Profanity Bestows Modesty

Profanity bestows modesty
in myself there's no grumbling or discontent
ah, were I to exhaust one million hands
even God would laugh
at a plight like that
should the situation demand
I would again go on a pilgrimage.

The time has been fulfilled, and God's kingdom is near
all of you repent, believe in the Good News
Ah, I'll take the shape of a female Sarutobi Sasuke[6]
and cross over volcanic craters, fly up into the sky
raising sprays of blood, I will fight
is the Good News like the sound of thunder?
I humbly ask.

Morning Mist Whiter Than a Ship

Morning mist whiter than a ship[7]
a glass stone of distant tears
stones from the core of the cruel earth
even a winter flower would freeze, I say
this monochrome of cold flesh
raises its voice in the swirling wind
walking alone, I'm simply walking.

Like the muddy depths of dirty water
no one can laugh
at the weakness of my stomach
I wrap my thoughts around me like a shawl
and demand an answer from god about this uncertain
        world.

If indeed the human world will turn to ashes
our pent-up breath, too, will disappear
drifting along, up and down
I sing out that I love a man
and the fires of hell resound
accompanying my harsh breathing.

There is no one who even cares
there's no use waiting forever
the beans of this floating world pop open
a fleeting moment, glass from the earth's core
glass from the earth's core shining, gushing forth.

The Fat Moon Has Vanished

The fat moon has vanished
carried off by a devil
hats on their heads everyone looked up at the sky.
A person licking his fingers
someone smoking a pipe
children shouting
in the dark sky the wind howls.

A lonely cough resonates from someone's windpipe
the blacksmith kindles his fire
the moon has gone somewhere.
Hail falls the size of spoons
the wrangling begins.

On a wager we went to look for the moon
and it's been tossed into a stove somewhere,
people clamour and shout.
Now, how long will it be
before people forget the moon and go on living?

Aizome Festival

At the Aizome festival
crowded with street performers
white Korean candy covered with flour
fireflies for sale, insects for sale
full applause for the street magicians
candy ices
cowards out for a walk
smelly carbide lamps
the banana vendor's twisted headband,
yes, that fat one is rotten.

Gramaphones with rubber listening tubes
I wonder if there's a poem by Homer
an evening like edelweiss flowering in a mountain recess,
sucking up water from the cotton, grass seeds sprout
                    green
a cluster of water flowers in a cup
like alpine plants
there's not one stall that is selling men
like a dry whelk whistle bright red[8]
my heart silent, I walk on.

Ah, if I had five more hours
what sort of person would come along, I wonder
I draw back into the impossible
little by little the color of my thoughts change
I suck hard sesame candies
I'm like a treasure chest destined to have no ties.

Two-Sen Copper Coin

You two-*sen* copper coin covered in blue mold!
Two-*sen* copper coin I picked up in front of the cowshed
you're big, heavy, sweet when I taste you
I can see in you a pattern like a coiled snake
minted in Meiji 34
that's a long time ago, isn't it
I was not even born yet.

Ah, it makes me happy to touch you
you feel like I can buy anything with you
I can buy a bean-jam bun
four big taffy candies, too
I'll polish you with ash until you sparkle
removing the grime of history
I hold you on the palm of my hand and gaze at you.

You're really like a gold coin
sparkling two-*sen* copper coin
I'll make you into a paperweight
or put you over my naked belly button
You two-*sen* copper coin that lets me play with you so
            intimately!

113

Notes

1. A famous wood block print by Katsushika Hokusai (1760-1849) depicts a red Mt. Fuji. As a symbol of Japan, Mt. Fuji seems to fare rather poorly in the texts of modern Japanese women poets. Similar to Hayashi, Fukao Sumako takes a critical look at the mountain in her poem, "Lone Beautiful Mount Fuji" (*O-hitori o-utsukushii o-Fuji-san*, 1949) in *Fukao Sumako senshū* (Tokyo: Shinjūsha, 1970), pp. 149-156. Sumako begins:

> "Eh? Mount Fuji you say?
> Not interesting in the least
> in the cruelly cold mirror of winter
> your classic white "new-look"
> Disgusts me, who're you trying to imitate? . . ."

Interestingly, Sumako treats the mountain as a hypocritical female, while Hayashi's Mt. Fuji seems to be of male gender.

2. The Taishō Emperor was mentally incompetent due to a childhood ailment and had to be replaced by his son as prince regent in 1921. The death of Taishō occurred in 1925.

3. An eighteenth century French romance by Abbé Prévost d'Éxiles, Manon Lescaut is the story of beautiful Manon who treats her lovers with a callous but charming disregard similar to that expressed in this poem. Another translation of this poem may be found in "Vagabond's Song" by Elizabeth Hanson in *To Live and To Write: Selections by Japanese Women Writers 1913-1938*, page 106.

4. A *yukata* is an unlined summer kimono of light cotton material with brightly colored designs.

5. A well-known Kabuki play.

6. Sarutobi Sasuke was a legendary master of *ninjutsu*, famous for his acrobatic, monkey-like leaps.

7. Another translation of this poem appears in "Vagabond's Song" in *To Live and To Write: Selections by Japanese Women Writers 1913-1938*, translated by Elizabeth Hanson, page 122.

8. The reference is to *umihozuki*, or the soft egg-case of the whelk, used by children as a whistle or noisemaker.

Part III

Reading *I Saw A Pale Horse*

Reading Fumiko's collection as a progression brings an awareness of each poem not only as particular and distinct but also as related to other poems in the text in a way or ways that contribute to a sense of the unfolding or development of meaning. At the same time, we might expect to find further evidence of progression in the relatedness of image and motif, theme, and/or other types of associative elements, and indeed, this does seem to be the case. However, such a reading cannot exhaust the possibilities of the text, and in fact, should encourage other, diverse readings. The intention of reading Fumiko's collection by progression and association, then, is an invitation to the text and to a reading of the female subject constructed therein.

"I Saw a Pale Horse": Breaking With the Phantoms of the Past

Fumiko's early writings, in general, foreground both physical presence and personal experience. "Preface," the poem which opens the *I Saw a Pale Horse* collection, is no exception. In this poem, Fumiko places her poetic subject center stage, body aged and gendered by frequent repetition of the phrase: "the twenty-five-year-old woman." This, as much as other subsequent self-referencing throughout the collection, marks Fumiko's collection as distinctly autobiographical in nature and in intent.[1] Declaring herself as subject, however, is only the beginning; imparting agency and significance to that subject is clearly another matter. "Preface," in spite of its initiating, declaratory position, is a writing of confusion and contradiction—the poet's words are mere "babble;" her sentiment erratic. The tensions generated by the contradictions of the poet's desire produce a restlessly speaking/stirring female subject seemingly incapable of finding direction. The poet's passion nonetheless spills over, encompassing the millet field itself, the grains of corn, the millet leaves; all become implicated in the poet's desire. The metaphor of body/millet field evokes what appears to be the initial stages of a process of volatile change and transformation. Thus, appropriating the unrelenting fecundity of the millet field, the poet entertains the promise of growth even as she harbors the anxiety of failure and of decline. Linking her primal utterances to the growing grains of corn, the poet seems determined that her words will take seed and grow. If such tiny grains may eventually grow to be one whole ear of corn, then perhaps, too, the seemingly insignificant babble of the poet's words will one day form a poetic 'body,' a text. Just as "one pitiful ear of corn" thrusts itself upward, so will the twenty-five-year-old woman. As much as "Preface" focuses on indecision and constraint, it also takes as subtexts the quest for autonomy and self-construction as well as the need for articulation of desires hitherto unspeakable and unspoken. Alone with feelings of agony and despair, the twenty-five-year-old woman gradually shapes the 'babble' of her words into meaningful queries, questions that will be taken up throughout the rest of the collection—shall she live or shall she die? shall she do this/shall she do that? In this explanatory first poem, Fumiko endows her peotic persona with body and voice, giving vent to frustration and dissatisfaction, and in so doing, inaugurates the *jo*, or introduction, that sets forth the principal themes and anxieties of the poet as she embarks upon a path leading to the construction of a textual subjectivity.

In a move that defers this inaugural moment, however, the poet does not immediately press forward, but, instead, compounds the contradictory pose of determination and indecision that marks "Preface" and turns back to the past. In this next poem, "I Saw a Pale Horse," the title poem of the collection, Fumiko pursues ghostly memories brought to life through the haunting figure of a pale horse:

> " . . . In the midst of a scene I have begun to forget
> walking dejectedly
> one pale horse!
> ah, it has begun to disappear a little now
> from my field of vision
> pale horse!"

The movement from the landscape of the millet field to the distant barn of the poet's childhood maintains the stifling, rural situation, yet the gaze of the twenty-five-year-old woman is now transformed into the viewpoint of a personal "I." Perspective shifts as the third-person "pre-face" gives way to the first-person 'face' of the poet. Similar to the twenty-five-year-old woman who attempts to find answers to her questions in a millet field, this "I" focuses on a country setting. Here, a dilapidated barn becomes the site of the poet's pain, and the symbol of that pain, an old pale horse. Pointing to some familial bond, something kept hidden from view, something the poet would forget but cannot, the pale horse weaves in and out of the poet's vision.

As a marker of birth, background, and family, the pale horse seems bound to draw the poet back into the old roles of dutiful daughter, beloved child, village girl. Yet the poet frantically resists:

" . . . All you dizzying noises, go away!
Shall I ride the pale horse,
threading my way through the trees around that
    deserted house?!
In the midst of this abundant nostalgia
stupid! stupid! stupid!
in the window of the police cell
I smell the distant barn."

In a violent denunciation of the pale horse, the poet turns her back on the prisonhouse of memory and, seizing her red *Diary of a Vagabond* notebook, flees the constrictions of home and family.

The motif of the white or pale horse gained currency in late Taishō Japan due primarily to the popularity of the autobiographical writings of the Russian anarchist, Boris Savinkov (1879-1925). Fumiko's poem and poetry collection, which makes use of this motif, has been traced to similar titles used by Savinkov.[2] Another Taishō poet, Hagiwara Sakutarō (1886-1942), also seems to have been attracted to this image, evoking a pale horse in his poem of that title in his *Blue Cat (Aoneko)* colection of 1923.[3] Fumiko's *aouma*, or pale horse is similar to that of Sakutarō, calling up a half-seen other world, a horse of dream, or memory. In Fumiko's case, the pale horse also hints at matters too painful to write. The precise reasons for the poet's flight from the village of the pale horse are not expressly stated, yet the determination to sever all ties with the parental home is powerfully evinced. In the poem "The Horse Wore An Ornamental Hairpin" from *Diary of a Vagabond*, Fumiko goes further, writing the horse as self/subject, a creature born to drudgery and endless servitude, unable to escape its pitiful fate. In both poems, the image of the horse works to reify the karmic load of the poet, a burden that in "I Saw a Pale Horse" is thrown off, rejected. Yet, the poet's search for freedom and fulfillment is immediately problematised; in leaving her village behind, has she simply exchanged one prison for another? and if so, will she ever be free?

The poet pursues this train of thought in the next poem, "Red Ball" (*Akai mari*), where the aspiring female diarist of "I Saw a Pale Horse" becomes a red ball tossed about by the wind. Soaring in the sky, directionless, the vagabond diarist is released from the physical body. The static image of the red diary in the previous poem is replaced by the dynamism of the red ball. Yet the pleasure of unrestrained freedom is cut short as the poet discovers the red ball, a mere plaything, has no will of its own. Indeed, the insouciant red ball soon finds itself

"Under the Lantern" (*Rantan no kage*), waiting tables in a cheap bar. Just as the red ball was tossed about by the wind, so too, is the inebriated waitress of this poem buffeted from customer to customer:

> " . . . How'm I doing? you ask
> I'm just fine
> although I'm a nice girl
> a really nice girl
> I scatter my feelings
> generously like cut flowers
> among petty pigs of men . . . "

In a link that connects the waywardness of red ball and waitress, the poet inscribes her body as object, a plaything of the moment; she remains a "nice girl" who must continue to look to the wind for release. The role of working woman, like that of the diarist/vagabond, brings no agency, only trivialization. Besieged by doubt, the poet turns for the first time to another for support, demanding love and affection from "Lord Buddha" (*Oshaka-sama*). Here, the frenzy of "Under the Lantern" is re-directed and re-channelled as the poet continues to seek escape, demanding a relationship so passionate that the self may be overwhelmed, subsumed in another:

> "I've fallen in love with Lord Buddha
> when I kiss his cool lips
> ah, I'm so undeserving
> my heart is benumbed.
>
> So unworthy am I
> from head to toe
> my calm blood flows against its tide
> seated on the lotus
> so composed and graceful
> his manly bearing
> bewitches my soul . . . "

Eroticism and the celebration of romantic love have long been the hallmarks of Japanese women's poetry, and in this respect, Fumiko has much in common with women writers of the past. Like Yosano Akiko, Fumiko gives voice to desire in language that extols the corporeality of physical love. Accordingly, she is not the first to remark on the charms of the Buddha figure. Similar to Fumiko, Akiko in her tanka collection *Tangled Hair* (*Midaregami*, 1901) also praises the beauty of Lord Buddha:

Only the sculptor's fame
Attracted me
When young,
But how exquisite now
The Buddha's face![4]

Both poets took inspiration from human models, in both cases a male poet, Akiko writing about her husband, Yosano Tekkan (1873-1935), and Fumiko about Okamoto Jun, or as some speculate, Tanabe Wakao. Further, both Akiko and Fumiko openly admire the physical beauty of the Buddha. Here, however, the similarities end. Akiko employs the classical tanka form to contemplate the face whereas Fumiko seeks the physical body, kissing the Buddha on the lips and begging for carresses in return. Unlike Akiko, she demands a response from the object of her affections. "Leap into my flaming breast," she cries, oblivious to all but her own desire. Fumiko's voice is that of an insistent and impetuous lover, set apart from Akiko by her choice of the lengthier *shi* format, the vigour of her language, and a deft ironic wit. Unfortunately, in spite of her passionate declaration, Lord Buddha remains silent. In this caustic portrayal of a masculine figure, the male 'god' neither listens to Fumiko's supplication nor acknowledges her presence. Similar to the scathing treatment of Mt. Fuji in "I've Seen Fuji" from *Diary of a Vagabond*, Lord Buddha appears much less impressive when viewed with the female eye. The poet will have to seek elsewhere for solace.

Fumiko continues to elaborate the lack of human connection in "Returning Home" (*Kikyō*) and in "Lament" (*Kurushii uta*). Here, however, the poet no longer expects change to be wrought by an outside agency. Rapidly losing her patience with the constrictions of society and gender, she now steps firmly outside the polite world of the "fortunate ones." Raising her voice in exclamation, pertinacious and rudely defiant, she gives vent to the explosive forces of resistance that continually simmer just beneath the surface of her text:

" . . . Although I spit blood and die in agony
the earth certainly won't stop in its tracks
they are preparing healthy bullets
one after another
in the show window
there is freshly baked bread
ah, how lightly beautiful like the sound of a piano
is the world I've never known.

Then all at once
I feel like crying out: goddammit!"

Her scream of rage, worthy of the anarchist poets, gives the first measure of release to the tension engendered by the first part of the collection. This angry voice of protest reverberates in "Heavy Heart" (*Tsukareta kokoro*), the final poem of the section, where the image of a cawing crow continues to foreground the poet's growing sense of rupture and discord.

With this first group of poems, then, the poet rouses herself from the state of indecision and lethargy in which she found herself in the millet field and posits possible answers to the shall-she-do-this-shall-she-do-that conundrum. Devoted daughter, female vagabond/poet, woman in love, working woman—each role offers a place for the "I," a means of living in the world, an answer to the "helpless confusion" of the twenty-five-year-old woman of "Preface." Presenting herself in various roles and in diverse physical postures, the poet seeks identity, relationship, fulfillment, meaning. Yet, one path does not seem preferable to another. At best, all seem questionable. Nonetheless, with a keen, self-regarding eye, the poet clearly sets forth the directions her life might take. She announces her presence and declares her difference. As such, these seven poems, along with "Preface," read as *jo*, or initial statement of the collection, functions as an introductory section that prepares the way for further amplification.

"Buying Sea Bream" and "Dear Katyusha:" The Fumiko Poetic Subject as Outsider

In these two central sections of the collection, the poet continues to focus on the flesh and blood female body. At the same time, enlarging the scope of the progression in the manner of the *ha*, she begins to develop the thematic interests set forth in the first eight poems. In "Buying Sea Bream" (*Tai o kau*), the poet strides through Tokyo, the streets resounding heartily with her newly awakened poetic voice: "damn it!/ laugh! laugh! laugh!" No longer content with the self-reflective monologic utterances of "Preface" and "I Saw a Pale Horse" or the one-sided petitioning of "Lord Buddha," the poet foregrounds her own speech, engaging in dialogue with shop boys and her female friend Tai-san, for whom the poem is written. She also invents conversations for her parents in the country. In a wild burst of loquacity, only hinted at in "Under the Lantern" and "Lament," the poet engages in excited talk that appears almost manic after the sombre tone of "Heavy Heart." The poet now *demonstrates* the impossibility of keeping silent, words flow from her mouth, break through the city sky, challenge the flying gulls. Poverty and destitution no longer deny her the power of speech. The outsider has begun to tell her story.

Whether wandering the streets of Tokyo in "Buying Sea Bream" or indulging in a sustained shout of grievance in "I Want to Say How Senseless It All Is" (*Baka o iitai*), the poet now gives full voice to her sense of powerlessness, and rails against it. She also begins to take steps to change her circumstances, to gain control over her body and her life. Most significantly, in the first of these central sections, she separates from her male partner. The unresponsive male figure portrayed in "Lord Buddha" has here become even less admirable. "Slippery as a sea cucumber" is the poet's simile in "Sobering Up" (*Yoizame*) as she continues to connect the phallic with treachery. Unfaithful lovers continue to be derided in "Love Is in the Heart" (*Koi wa nume sanzun no uchi*), "The Queen's Homecoming" (*Joosama no okaeri*), and in "Taking Out the Liver" (*Ikigimedori*) where the poet imagines murder, peering into the sliced-open belly of the man who has deserted her.

Reading the first poems of Fumiko's collection no doubt gives some indication of what lies behind Tōmaru Tatsu's figurative 'axe in the head' remark quoted earlier. Vehemence is indeed a principal feature encountered in Fumiko's use of language. Even in translation, Fumiko's dynamism is not lost. Dotted with expletives, invective, exclamations, Fumiko's poetry is far from delicate and restrained. The verbal attack continues as the collection progresses, the reader at times seemingly buttonholed by a madwoman, importuned by a drunk, or set upon by a fury. At other times, however, the poet ushers us into the lost, lonely world of childhood or admits us to her erotic dreams. Unrestrained, Fumiko leaps, swoops, cavorts, crying out in violent monologue, demanding reciprocation. The extremity of the poet's circumstances seem well matched by the extremity of language and feeling. Allied with the tendency towards hyperbole is the poet's propensity for figurative language employing bold, violent, corporeal imagery, such as that of the lover's heart in "Lord Buddha" which is "like a broken bee's nest," or the sliced open belly of the unfaithful lover in which a killfish swims in "Taking Out the Liver." Yet the sting of the wild harangue is often deflected by a dash of humor, a touch of comic bravado as the poet reveals a good-natured self-irony that, frequently, gestures to her resistance as theatrical act, and thus allays the over-all tone of anger and despair. " . . . (H)ear ye, hear ye!/the final scene with that man has come slowly but surely . . . " she intones in "Taking Out the Liver," distancing herself from the painful event in mock-heroic perfomance.

In "Lone Journey" (*Hitori tabi*), however, the poet suppresses this urge to brighten her existence:

> " . . . Ah, I'd like to smoke a cigarette
> but even if I yell "Wo!"
> the wind will carry my voice away
> in the white sky
> the face of the man who has made me drink vinegar
> is so big, so big.
>
> Ah, it's really lonely travelling alone."

Unlike her previous reactions to adversity, the poet now holds her dissenting voice in check. There is no one to hear her shout; no one to whom speech can be directed. Should she call out, her words will be lost in a vast emptiness. Only one image fills her vision, that of the man who has treated her badly. The realization that she may be outside and beyond the bounds of meaningful discourse brings the poet to a new consideration of her solitary life, one which she pursues throughout the rest of this section. In "Good Demon, Bad Demon" (*Zenma to akuma*), for example, the poet reconsiders her desire for human contact. Is companionship simply a battle of opposing desires? "Good Demon, Bad Demon" offers no answers as the shared cigarette gives way to the taste of ashes in the next poem, "Dwarf in the Ashes" (*Hai no naka no kobito*), a link that maintains the descent into a hell of loneliness. In this poem, and the next, "Heart of Autumn" (*Aki no kokoro*), the poet continues to examine her isolated existence, juxtaposing the hellish and the idyllic, two contradictory aspects of her solitary life. On one hand, in "Dwarf," loneliness stunts one's growth and brings mind-numbing misery:

> " . . . as I was staring at the ashes in the brazier
> on top of the uneven surface
> a dwarf came stepping along
> carrying a bag like poppy seed.
>
> —There's nothing to worry about, lady
> poor people are lucky, he said, heh, heh
> Ah, I was so tired
> and so sad I began to cry . . . "

while, on the other hand, in "Heart of Autumn," the poet's lonely life ensures peace and contentment:

> " . . . In the blue medicine bottle
> the light of the red lantern
> flickering, flickering
> the lovers who pass through the town
> waving their walking sticks
> I shall put into an old match box
> and like a young girl
> wind them round and round . . . "

> " . . . Autumn is fine
> both day and night
> my life stretches on like a rail."

Eventually, both hellish and idyllic seem to merge in "Kiss" (*Seppun*), as the poet dispels the mellow mood of her autumn journey with the memory of an almost demonic embrace:

> "The night I first kissed
> the cherries were blooming under the lanterns
>
> the moon was red—
>
> his lips, which seemed as if they would suck blood
> even in parting
> even in parting
> on his lips the moon danced round and round."

In "Kiss," the poet shifts her focus from the peaceful melancholy of an autumn evening to the mesmerizing sensuality of a spring night, contrasting the natural beauty of the two most preferred seasons in Japan in a move reminiscent of classical linked poetry. Thus, the lanterns that coolly flickered in the glass of the blue medicine bottle in "Heart of Autumn" glow with a carnal light in "Kiss," where they dye the moon red. Further, as the clarity of autumn merges into the warm haziness of spring, the promenading lovers the poet would capture in "Heart of Autumn" become in "Kiss" the poet herself ensnared by passion. The calm self-reflexivity of the autumnal poem is challenged by the vampiric spell of the lover's kiss, a kiss so captivating the poet imagines losing all sense of equilibrium. Yet, Fumiko is quick to re-assert her single state with a pun: have her lover's lips parted in passion or have the lovers parted from each other? Linking the romantic atmosphere of lips parting in a kiss to the harsh reality of utterance, the poet critiques female sentimentality in "Words of a Romantic" (*Romanchisuto no kotoba*). Here, the poet tells us that women are eager victims of romance, never protesting, enduring every outrage. In a reversal of traditional values, the poet sees this not as strength but as weakness. Women are weak, not because they are women, but because they accept their roles. They believe they cannot live alone; they accept poverty; they expect betrayal; they live only for the passionate kiss; they accept the beating.

The witty honesty of "Words of a Romantic" as well as the struggle of the female subject to accustom herself to life on her own is intensified in "A Clear View" (*Hogarakunaru fūkei*), the final poem of the first *ha* section. Here, the determined bravado of the romantic optimist once again becomes the tortured self-reflection of the outcast. Ostracized by society and denied relationship due to her poverty and marginal status, the poet finds herself pushed aside by the crowd. Yet, unlike the seething figure in "Lament" who can only cry out in frustration, the poet here launches a direct attack upon her abusers. In so doing, her anger and bitterness are released; sweet winds blow from her mouth:

> . . . "The pleasures of honest living
> are not to tell lies and to eat white rice every day
> "So Fumiko is lucky!"
> Just once I want to shout that to someone."

For the first time, a named identity appears. Indeed, a lessening of anger accompanies the emergence of the name, Fumiko, from the text. Alone but less fragmented, vulnerable but less in doubt, the poet seems prepared to move in a new direction. Identity is about to be re-worked and reconstituted, a task undertaken in the second *ha* section, "Dear Katyusha" (*Itoshi no Kachyūsha*).

A story-poem divided into seven parts, "Dear Katyusha," the title poem of this section, is the longest of the entire collection. Undertaking a new direction and also a new format, the poet embarks upon the re-invention of the poetic subject with a return to the childhood past. In this poem, we follow a twelve-year old peddler girl as she makes her rounds, selling ten-*sen* fans on a hot August day. Images of Katyusha, the tragic herione of Tolstoy's novel *Resurrection* are everywhere—the name of the song, the name of a pretty foreign girl in a poster, a word on the lips of the roughest miner.[5] When the miners begin to call the young girl herself "Katyusha," she is overjoyed. Full of hope, she decides to struggle on. A simple tale, perhaps, but a tale nonetheless, as the poet begins a re-negotiation, a re-inscription of the *Pale Horse* collection as personal poetic narrative.

Very different from the old home envisaged in "I Saw a Pale Horse" or "Returning Home," the town of Nōgata in "Dear Katyusha" is a coal-mining village. Nostalgia for the past centers on the figure of Katyusha rather than on the hardships of the peddling life or on the parents who are now identified frankly as "step-father and mother" rather than the "father and mother" of the earlier poems about the "old village." Thus, life in Nōgata is invested with a much less mysterious, idealizing vision than that of "I Saw a Pale Horse." In Nōgata, for example, there are brothels, dirty tenements, a miners' strike. Above these things, however, shines the figure of Katyusha, with whom the peddler girl strongly identifies, to the extent of copying the foreign girl's hairstyle and drawing her face repeatedly in her notebooks. Through her memories of Katyusha, the poet recovers not only the colorful reality of her childhood but also comes to entertain the possibility of self-transformation. Perceived by the miners as Katyusha, the peddler girl proceeds at once to recreate herself in the image of this fictional figure:

> " . . . When I returned to our lodging house
> I parted my hair and gave myself Katyusha's hairstyle.
> Dear Katyusha . . . .
> but I was a poor girl who knew nothing
> holding onto vast hopes

> I grew up
> like a vegetable box onion."

As a childish Katyusha look-alike, the poet realizes she once transcended the bounds of her squalid existence. As an adult who now casts her eyes back on the past, the poet is aware that her fantasy both protected her from and blinded her to the harsh circumstances of her life. In spite of life in the vegetable box, the old vision did bring growth and strength. What of new visions? Pursuing further the notion of transformation found in "Dear Katyusha," the poet returns to the present, now actively seeking new directions, even a new "body."

In the poems which follow, "The Town Where One Can't See the Sea" (*Umi no mienai machi*), "Sweetheart" (*Jōjin*), and "Passion for Snow" (*Yuki ni yoseru netsujō*), the poet imagines actual physical transformations, linking together poems in which the body of the poetic subject acquires fantastic guise. Although these figures, like Katyusha, represent transformations of the physical shape, such fictions lack that specific grounding in experience that gives Katyusha her powerful appeal. Ultimately, such attempts at reconstruction give way to the onslaught of the lived life, as in the following poems, "Woman Dead Drunk" (*Yoidore onna*) and "My Ship Has Sailed" (*Noridashita fune dakedo*), where the poet seems to worry that she, too, like the unhappy Katyusha, may be unable to achieve her hopes and dreams. In "My Ship Has Sailed," the poet cries out in shocked realization:

> " . . . Until I die I'll be a cafe waitress, maid, factory
> > girl
> worthless woman
> I'll have to die working! . . ."

All those fantasies of love, power, beauty so many false hopes; the assumed personae of peddler girl, woman betrayed, vagabond poet, dutiful daughter, mermaid, sphinx meaningless beside the harsh reality of existence. Her search for meaning/subjectivity has led her in a circle. To break that circle the poet must reach more deeply within, the "body" must be somehow reborn, the subject re-written:

> " . . . arrows, bullets, fly to me
> in front of these disgusting men and women
> I want to show you Fumiko's bowels."

For the Fumiko poetic subject, true self-transformation requires more than donning a costume or adopting a role, it demands more than a superficial probing. The revitalization of her life must proceed from the very roots of her being, hence the visceral exposé that affects traditional *seppuku*. Attempting to divest herself of all false 'bodies,' she exposes her true 'flesh,' the hidden inner workings of her physical core. From this pared-down vision of self, she undertakes to re-construct her poetic 'body.'

In "Red Slipper" (*Akai surippa*), the poet hesitates, apparently overwhelmed by the task she has set herself. Similar to the irresolution that marks "Preface" and "I Saw a Pale Horse," the poet once again pauses before moving forward. Up until this point, anger, frustration, despair have driven her, provided the poetic spark, fueled the compilation of the collection. Now, the poet tells us, courage is what the female subject needs to move on, but her "cowardly hand still clings to the swivel chair." Releasing oneself from habit, even from the habit of misery, seems an enormously difficult task. One means of escape may be to fall asleep, as in "Preface," but the momentum of the collection now precludes such a possibility. The poet is compelled by her own construct to continue: " . . . slap my face as hard as you can/and knock off my other slipper, too . . . " she demands, with a resurgence of the old boldness. Bringing the *ha* sections of her collection to a close, Fumiko turns her red slipper of slavery into the red tide of revolution as she sets out on her final course.

"Red Sails Gone to Sea": Freedom, Work, and the Struggle for Relationship

The slipper which flies from the poet's foot in "Red Slipper" now lends its color to the sails of ships manned by disgruntled factory workers in "Red Sails Have Gone to Sea" (*Shuho wa umi e deta*). Focusing on a shipbuilders' strike on the island of Innoshima near Onomichi, Fumiko allies her own poetic endeavour with the proletarian struggle for freedom. In keeping with the quickening pace of the *kyū*, the six poems of this final section move at a much accelerated rate, reaching towards resolution. "Red Sails," with its emphasis on power and the transfer of power, is well-chosen as the poem which begins this last important section. Enjoining the reader to listen to "the sound of the vast wide sea," or to "the roar of the waves," the poet's voice resounds vigorously, backed by the power of the ocean. Although previously in the collection the sea has evoked contradictory images of freedom and destruction or dissolution, in "Red Sails," its great energy is harnessed to the control of inimical forces and the accomplishment of desire. For the poet, the sea now inspires action and courage.

As the poet describes the actions of the rebellious workers, their undertaking soon appears analogous to Fumiko's own. Highlighting the rising tension of the strike in a manner similar to the progression of the collection which has focused on the growing realization of the poetic subject, the poet begins with a scene of vaguely unhappy workers kicking pebbles along the beach. She then traces the slow building of emotion which is finally fanned into a fury as the workers batter down the gates of the factory and pursue the fleeing bosses into the ocean. Very similar to the overall movement of *I Saw a Pale Horse*, this poem proceeds from an initial sense of uneasiness located within an individual body or bodies, builds steadily to an extreme state of tension and dissatisfaction and, as the significance of incident and event becomes clear, produces an explosive outburst that utterly transforms the original entity. Conclusion follows in a quieter vein. Placing "Red Sails" at this juncture provides not only an effective iteration of the dynamic rhythms of the collection but also points towards some sort of resolution, as the poet observer reflects upon a progression of events, signified through the agency of the human body, that seems to parallel her own emotional cognition.

In "Red Sails," the sudden decision of the workers to take action is a source of inspiration to the poet's persona who is herself unable to act in the previous poem, "Red Slipper." The image of the red sails, even though torn and mouldering, becomes a symbol of reckless courage in the face of impossible odds, a powerful alternative for the cowardly figure of "Red Slipper." Nonetheless, the poet chooses to leave us not with an image of the daring workers but of the wives and children who must wait behind on shore, their voices "vigorous as the waves," their eyes filled with the reflection of the red sails "speeding along like sparks of fire." Courage, it seems, is subject to certain essentialist criteria. Men leave, women stay. Letting go the swivel chair or vanishing into the middle of the ocean may constitute an act of courage, yet these are acts which the poet does not see fit to undertake. The female social body is not abandoned, the situation at hand is not ignored. Just as Fumiko preferred to eschew the extremes of the anarcho-dadaist poets who sought to leave the old language behind and explore other realms, and in company with other women writers of Taishō-early Shōwa who wrote with a keen awareness of social issues, the poet here, too, elects to remain on shore, feet solidly planted on the ground, her voice raised clearly in protest, closely allied with the homely concerns of the waving women and children.

The decision to remain involved in the mundane female world in spite of its imperfections and disappointments and further to continue to articulate the female position is a major commitment for the poet. Having written her self and body, having laid bare her desires, frustrations, fears, and disappointments, the poet now moves towards resolution. As she undertakes to implement her newly realized subjectivity, the final poems of *I Saw a Pale Horse* undergo a marked change in tone and content. In the first of these, "Quiet Heart" (*Shizugokoro*), the poet engages in the actual construction of a literary artefact, a story for children, which she completes at the dawn of a new day:

> "It's late at night
> in the distance the cock is calling
> tomorrow I shall buy rice with this
> a fine children's story I have written
> at my mandarin orange box desk
> if I can get some money for it

> my daydreams will vanish in the pure white electric light
> that illuminates the night . . ."

Her patient effort as well as the story she produces recall the children who keep their vigil on the mountain in "Red Sails." Needless to say, the poet takes great pleasure in her new accomplishment. Pride and satisfaction are further reflected in the pleasant anticipation of filling her stomach, the first time we have seen the poet actually preparing to eat, not simply craving that which she cannot have. Hungry though she is, and as destitute as she seems, the former anger and frustration are no longer in evidence. The old emotions have been replaced with a feeling of warm contentment and the possibility of new beginnings, born out in the description of herself as "happy as a baby," and represented significantly in the motif of a completed text. Her "work" is no longer in the cafes, but here in her own room, at her mandarin orange box desk upon which she writes, producing a saleable article which satisfies both financially and emotionally. The past, like the narcissus, is quickly fading; daydreams of the future are fast becoming present reality.

The woman writer of "Quiet Heart," quick to dispose of all that binds her to the past, tosses her old love letters into the fire of the next poem, "Burn!" (*Moerō!*), in a link that seems to destroy the love letters and, indeed, anything that smacks of sadness and regret. The burning sparks that kindle the new fire in her heart as well as the image of the poet's "child-like" heart alighting atop a large tree continue to allude to the watchful stance of the women and children under the withered tree of "Red Sails." Yet, in this poem, the sparks of fire are no longer reflections of a courageous act but the means of igniting the poet's passion for self-renewal. In "Burn!", the impression is one of freedom and release rather than that of the barely contained forbearance of "Red Sails."

The fire of happiness and freedom continues to burn in the next poem, "Chain of Sparks" (*Hibana no kusari*) as the poet conjures up a journey with her lover:

> " . . . I wished I had a red shawl
> if I had put on that red shawl
> in the lightly, silently falling snow
> and went on a trip with my lover . . . "

Recalling "Preface" where the twenty-five-year-old woman yearned for a male lover and the freedom to travel, two desires which seemed mutually exclusive, "Chain of Sparks" joins these twin hopes in a dazzling blend of images that conflate the earlier figure of Katyusha with that of the poetic persona washing rice in a frozen field. The juxtaposition of this exceedingly domestic task with the image of a red shawl and travelling with one's lover in lightly falling snow gives the Katyusha motif a decidedly new twist. Here, unlike Katyusha, the poetic subject does not rap helplessly at train windows; neither does she travel alone. Instead, she prepares food, the icy coldness of the task preparatory to the warmth of physical satisfaction. Allowing her anticipation to run along like a train at full speed, the romantic fantasy turns into a power-packed dynamo, "burning like a chain of sparks." Thus, although the figure of Katyusha continues to inform the poet's self-image, it has lost much of its earlier passivity; galvanized by the vitality of the subject herself, the image of the fictional heroine is re-generated, no longer a mere memory but a source of energy propelling the poet onward.

The poet's dream train of desire carries her into the surreal world of dream itself in "Dream While Unemployed" (*Shisshoku shite mita yume*), linking the poet's new energies to the excitement of sexual fantasy. In this penultimate poem, the poet offers a bizarre recapitulation of major thematic elements in the collection, compressed and distorted in the manner of the dream world. In a few lines, the poet retraces the wandering journey through life, work in a grueling job, sexual adventures and the promise of love, betrayal by her lover, their poverty. Attempting to flee over the sea, in an allusion to the sea-faring workers of "Red Sails," the poet pulls her persona up short, "bang! I lost my virginity," she declares, her body always the site upon which the poetic subject is inscribed and tested. Here, body/subject have come of age. The little grains of corn in "Preface" have at last matured, the vegetable box onion in "Dear Katyusha" has indeed grown right up. The vagabond-poet who ran away on a steamship in "I Saw a Pale Horse" is no longer a child. The hard-working woman of "Under the Lantern" and "Sobering Up" is no longer employed, or employable, in her former menial tasks. Seeking self-definition through work is no longer possible unless it is the work of writing, a fact realized at the conscious level in a poem like "Quiet Heart" and here on the deeper level of dream. With the loss of 'virginity,' the poet acknowledges not only an awakening to new life but also the end of the nightmare-like existence that has hitherto plagued her with its fantasy, false hopes, and mesmerizing allure.

In the final poem of the collection, "Flowers on a Moonlit Night" (*Tsukiyo no hana*), the poet transforms the frenetic dreamscape of "Dream While Unemployed" into the peaceful magicality of an ordinary world. Apropos of the *kyū*, or finale, the poet chooses to conclude on an auspicious note. Described by critics as "fairytale-like" or "folktale-like,"[6] "Flowers on a Moonlit Night" both reinforces and expands the dream imagery of the previous poem, particularly the treatment of female sexuality. Thus, the dream lover becomes a human lover, and the poet a 'wifely' companion instead of a sea-faring renegade.

Also, in a surprise move, the poet allows for the first time a sympathetic representation of a male figure. Unlike the uncommunicative figure of "Lord

Buddha," or the worthless partners of "Sobering Up" and "Taking Out the Liver," the poor painter of "Flowers on a Moonlit Night" speaks openly and honestly with the poet, recalling a glimpse he once had of a running fox. In Japanese folklore, the fox is believed to assume human female form, often that of bride or wife. The painter does not fear the fox's wild autonomy nor its gendered otherness; in fact, he appears to welcome it. For the poet, such an understanding partner appears to be a kind of "miracle," yet she hesitates to accept his trust. Instead, she puts forward her own self image, a pale flower that recalls the pale horse of the past, and dismisses the painter's fox from view in the final lines. Thus, even though the red flowers open enigmatically in the moonlight, suggesting the depth and compassion of the painter's love as well as the rich promise of a new self-unfolding for the poet, the poet still harbours reservations. Her 'happiness' lacks that earthy satisfaction and sense of personal accomplishment found in "Quiet Heart," or in the poem that concludes *Diary of a Vagabond*, "Two-sen Copper Coin." Whereas *I Saw a Pale Horse* concludes with an expanded focus on the two, the heterosexual couple, *Diary of a Vagabond* closes with an affirmation of the one, the woman alone. Fumiko thus entertains both possibilities—she seems determined to prove she can and will live either way. Although the gorgeous red flowers promise a new center for the female subject, these are nonetheless a gift, something given and not earned, something shared with another, and therefore, for the lone poet who thrives on her own self-constructions, always problematic.

With the exception of the poor painter, the portrayal of male figures in the collection up until now has been bitter and unflattering. Nonetheless, even though the poet has cast off abusive, uncaring male partners, she has not set aside hope for acceptance, for esteem, for alliance with the kind of partner Adrienne Rich calls the "Man-Who-Would-Understand."[7] In this final poem, Fumiko chooses the poor painter over a life lived alone, and thus connection over estrangement, relationship over solitude. Moreover, she also writes a male subject. The coming together of male and female in harmony and equality in "Flowers on a Moonlit Night," a conclusion that brings the collection to resolution, represents a slender strand that flows through Fumiko's works: the possibility of forming a new centre in which female and male are joined in mutuality. Perhaps alone among women writers of the period, Fumiko wrote successfully both female and male subjects.[8] Yet, in general, poems like "Lord Buddha," "Sobering Up," or "My Ship Has Sailed" more accurately represent Fumiko's later, fictional approach to female-male relationships: as disjunctive alliances that bring only anguish and torment.

To read Fumiko's later fictional works is to note not only such continuing thematics as the above, it is to realize that the thirty-four poems of *I Saw a Pale Horse* represent in suitably compressed form the seed from which all of Fumiko's subsequent fiction would grow. According to Hirabayashi Taiko, *I Saw a Pale*

Horse should be read as "the foundation of Hayashi Fumiko's literature"[9] while another critic concludes that this poetry collection "almost equals the weight of all the prose works written by Fumiko, including the early and late periods."[10] High praise indeed for *I Saw a Pale Horse*, and also, very clear statements of how deeply Fumiko's writing is invested by this early poetry collection. Moreover, such statements imply that Fumiko's poetic-autobiography, as a foundational writing, exhibits a certain development of thematic elements, production of motif and image, construction of subject and narrative progression familiar from the prose writings. If this is the case, then *I Saw a Pale Horse* may be considered further as a kind of proto-narrative that, with its emphasis on personal story, develops in a way that both anticipates the later prose writings and also determines their production.

Conclusion: Fumiko, the Poetic Subject, and Narrativization

In *I Saw a Pale Horse*, Fumiko took the events and experiences of her own life and body as the building blocks of a textual world and, writing against mainstream tradition, constructed a female poetic subject that gave order and meaning to the chaos of her own lived life. The textualization of this "life" was so successful that in time Fumiko built an extensive literary corpus based upon this one lone figure. Ironically, the powerful appeal of Fumiko's female poetic subject is derived from its very lack of power, from its positioning at the extreme edges of Japanese society. Whereas many Japanese women write from a similar acute position, few share Fumiko's radical bohemianism. By means of gender, background, and birth, Hayashi was doubly, even triply, marginalized. Her attempt to construct herself textually must be read against her outsider status as well as against problems of gender connected to Japanese literary practice.[11]

In Fumiko's case, exclusion from the center brought about in the poetic subject an interplay of two antagonistic positions, one in which the subject, overwhelmed by her desire for the center, does everything in her power to possess it, and another in which the subject realizes the center is denied her and so undertakes to make her own way, ignoring social and/or literary convention. Both of these contrasting factors are at work in *I Saw a Pale Horse*, and also in *Diary of a Vagabond*.

Understandably, the poet depicts a female subject who desires to burst the excruciating bonds of being poor, female, and a social outsider. While the poems of the collection deal directly with issues of poverty and gender, the social ostracism faced by the poet is less clearly defined. Often depicted at the mercy of others, that is, "they," "the fortunate ones," "the crowd," the "disgusting men and women," the poet sees herself as tormented by a wide range of people. Examining the relevant passages, we may easily conclude that she is despised by nearly all with whom she comes into contact. With the exception of the mother, of Tai-san, and of the poor painter, the poet allows her persona to form no bonds at all. Rather than interpreting this antagonism of others as due only to poverty (the primary reason given in the collection for this discrimination), we may read obliquely here the shadow of the poet's own illegitimacy, connoted by the haunting image of the pale horse and its connection to the hidden world of family ties. When the family situation is once again invoked in "Dear Katyusha" as the poet moves towards resolution, we find a more attractive, and at the same time more candid, representation of the outcast status. Excluded from the center, the poet now raises a figure that becomes central to and in itself. The very reason for exclusion becomes the means of poetic empowerment. It also becomes the means of experimenting with a created 'character' in a narrative-like format. "Dear Katyusha" represents a very early attempt at narrative by Fumiko, and while certainly other poems in the collection exhibit similar features (most notably, the title poems of each section: "I Saw a Pale Horse," "Buying Sea Bream," and "Red Sails Gone to Sea") and indeed the collection as a whole may be read as a kind of "emplotted" poetic progression, there is no other poem that possesses the same degree of narrativizing as "Dear Katyusha." In this sense, "Dear Katyusha" represents a potent conflation of narrative and poetic elements within the self-writing framework.

Through this figure of Katyusha (as well as through the other "I"s of the text), Fumiko reflects upon her own life and, in the constructing of her text, brings form and shape to that life; her poetic composition becomes, in fact, not only the transposing of the female body to language, as Enchi Fumiko observed, but the textual composing of a "life," the engendering of a "story." Beginning in "Preface" with a figure that lacks will, commitment, or design, the poet gradually builds through the arrangement of poems in her collection a persona that acquires the ability to make choices, a persona that obtains empowerment through self-writing. The narrativization of this self is Fumiko's response to the lack of a subject position in Japanese letters that would endorse women of the lower social orders who are both talented and able. Deprived of place, the outsider poet appropriates her own space as the place from which she will speak, the place from which she will tell her story. Assuming the stance of female outsider, Fumiko endows her poetic presence with its own exclusivity. Her lone position becomes the place wherein her uniqueness can be fully recognized and exploited, weakness being turned to power. As the poet succeeds in reconstructing herself and her life through text, she imparts to her readers a keen and powerful sense of accomplishment. Unlike her anarchist associates, Fumiko manages to give shape and significance to the confusion, chaos, and hopelessness of her life through her poetry.

The freedom of lower-class women to work, to write, to love, to live—all of these Fumiko addresses in *I Saw a Pale Horse* no less than in her later prose writings. In spite of the fact that Fumiko was neither "anarchist" nor "proletarian," the position from which she wrote established a confrontational critical stance. As Sidonie Smith observes in lines which seem especially pertinent to an understanding of Fumiko's poetry, particularly the "shock" value of that poetry: "Writing her experiential history of the body, the autobiographical subject engages in a process of critical self-consciousness through which she comes to an awareness of the relationship of her specific body to the cultural "body" and to the body politic. That change in consciousness prompts cultural critique."[12] Fumiko's writing the Japanese autobiographical subject as female outsider was an act that opened a new window on representations of Japanese women and Japanese society by Japanese women writers, helping to affirm and foster the possibility of alternative vision and voice.

Besides the preference for the female outsider as autobiographical narrative subject, the structuring of *I Saw a Pale Horse*, with its focus on self-discovery as well as on the female subject through which this process takes place, is found throughout Hayashi's fictional works, including *Diary of a Vagabond*. From the very first published prose work, "The Accordion and the Fish town" (*Fūkin to uo no machi*, 1931) to works of the mature, later years, such as *Floating Clouds* (*Ukigumo*, 1949), "Bones" (*Hone*, 1948), "Narcissus" (*Suisen*, 1949), "River Gudgeon" (*Kawahaze*, 1946) to name but a few, and also observable in Fumiko's last, unfinished work, *Meals* (*Meshi*, 1951), the structuring of the text is basically identical to that of this first poetry collection as outlined above, while in other stories, such as "Late Chrysanthemum" (*Bangiku*, 1948), the outsider figure of the poetry collection is reconstituted as fictional female figure attempting to come to terms with a life lived on the edge. It is as if the writer has a need to tell her story again and again, to constantly and continually legitimize her self/subject. Such an extrapolation is not meant to imply that Fumiko's later works are particularly formulaic. Simply stated, it is that these later narratives have running through them a distinct undercurrent that flows naturally and easily from the first poetry collection and marks these writings as characteristic of and closely affined to the poetic world of *I Saw a Pale Horse*. That this very early poetic formulation provided such fertile ground for Fumiko's experiment with a new female enunciative position and, further, possessed such intrinsic durability over the course of time is more than sufficient cause to read *I Saw a Pale Horse* not only as a formative first text by a major Japanese woman writer but also in its own right, as a major work of modern Japanese poetry.

Coming to writing through poetry, primarily because of the ease in jotting down random thoughts and feelings in the workaday world, Fumiko early developed an autobiographical poetry through which she attempted to resolve the difficulties of her life. Looking back over the ten years through which she had struggled to survive as a woman and as a poet, she assembled thirty-four poems that gave voice to her struggle and also, in retrospect, helped impart coherence and significance to that struggle. There is an awareness in the collection, then, of the female poetic subject as pose and also as process, as a constructed persona and also as a persona in the making. The interaction of these two areas, one centered on the presentation of a textual 'self', the other on the ever-changing, yet sequential nature of that self, propel and animate the collection, creating a fascinating montage that, like the art deco cover, offers two contrasting views that form and re-form about the other. From this interchange between pose and process, text and life, body and text emerges a dynamic personal statement, empowered and empowering, a poetic sourcebook for all of Hayashi Fumiko's literature.

Notes

1. The original edition of the collection contained two prefaces, one by socialist critic and thinker, Ishikawa Sanshirō (1876-1956), and one by Tsuji Jun. Fumiko herself also wrote a preface which is in fact this first poem. After the author's preface/poem came the table of contents, and *then* the first section containing seven poems, beginning with "I Saw a Pale Horse." The positioning of this preface/poem as well as its title gesture to the autobiographical. Fumiko was twenty-five years old in 1928; the preface/poem dated 1928/29 is the only poem in the collection to be so marked.

2. Mori, p. 17. Savinkov's works were *The Pale Horse* (*Kon'blednyi*, in Japanese translation *Aozametaru uma*, 1909) and *The Black Horse* (*Kon'voronoi*, 1923). The latter, entitled in Japanese *Kurouma o mitari* (*I Saw a Black Horse*), may also have influenced Fumiko's choice of title (see Mori, pp. 17-18). The Chinese character used for *ao* in the Japanese translation of the Savinkov title is the same as that chosen by Fumiko for her poetry collection; also, Savinkov's texts both were autobiographical writings (*The Black Horse* being a diary sequel to *The Pale Horse*).

3. Hagiwara Sakutarō, "Aozameta uma" in *Aoneko* in *Hagiwara Sakutarō zenshū*, vol. 1 (Tokyo: Chikuma shobō, 1986), pp. 197-198. In the Japanese language, the color *ao* covers a rather wide spectrum, depending on the Chinese character used and commonly accepted notions regarding the color of certain objects. *Ao* may be taken to mean anything from black or blue or green to white, gray, or simply as an absence of color, i.e., pale.

4. Sanford Goldstein and Seishi Shinoda, trans., *Tangled Hair: Selected Tanka from Midaregami*, by Yosano Akiko (Rutland, Vermont and Tokyo, Japan, Charles E. Tuttle, 1987), tanka 162, p. 107.

5. Katyusha is the name of the heroine of *Resurrection* (*Voskresenie*, 1899), a novel by Leo Tolstoy (1828-1910). Translated by Shimamura Hōgetsu (1871-1918) and made into a stage play in 1914, *Resurrection* (*Fukkatsu* in Japanese) was performed all over Japan, the female lead played by Matsui Sumako (d. 1919) whose rendition of the Katyusha song became emblematic of the early Taishō era.

6. Mori, p. 36.

7.Quoted by Marianne Hirsch in *The Mother/Daughter Plot: Narrative, Psychoanalysis, Feminism* (Bloomington and Indianapolis: Indiana University Press, 1989), pp. 57-58.

8. Some of the better known works by Fumiko that write the male subject are "The Oyster" (*Kaki*, 1935), "Crybaby" (*Nakimushi kozō*, 1934), and *Floating Clouds* (*Ukigumo*, 1949).

9. Tsuboi Sakae and Hirabayashi Taiko, "Hayashi Fumiko no omoide," *Gendai shi bunko: Hayashi Fumiko shishū*, p. 130.

10. Tōmaru, p. 147.

11. Although Japanese women writers, by virtue of the classical female literary tradition, are accorded a place in modern Japanese letters, their voice does not belong to the center. This was particularly true at the time when Fumiko began writing. Fumiko's self-construction may also be read against earlier prototypes of strong-willed, uneducated women to try to live for themselves, particularly those depicted in the works of Tokuda Shūsei (1871-1943). Shūsei, who acted as mentor to Fumiko during her early wandering years, was greatly admired by the young poet, and Fumiko strove to emulate this "master of naturalism" in her first attempts at prose fiction. According to James Fujii in his insightful study of the subject position in Japanese prose narrative, a typical Shūsei female protagonist could only attain success by moving "outside . . . socially structured paths. Difference . . . be(ing) the condition from which she would have to make her mark . . . " (See James A. Fujii, *Complicit Fictions: The Subject in the Modern Japanese Prose Narrative* (Berkeley: University of California Press, 1993), p. 217. While the Shūsei female subject seems to share with Fumiko the predisposition towrds "difference" as a means of achieving personal goals, Fumiko moved beyond Shūsei's representations with her exploitation of "difference" as writing strategy. Indeed, although modern women poets and writers in general can be said to have positioned themselves similarly, Fumiko's writing of the female subject remains one of the most flambuoyant.

12. Smith, p. 131.

APPENDIX

List Of Poems

I Saw a Pale Horse

Selected Poems from Diary of a Vagabond

Sources in English

Apter, David E., and James Joll, eds. *Anarchism Today*. London: Macmillan, 1971.

Bennett, Paula. *My Life a Loaded Gun: Female Creativity and Feminist Poetics*. Boston: Beacon Press, 1986.

Brodzski, Bella and Celeste Schneck, eds. *Life/Lifes: Theorizing Women's Autobiography*. Ithaca, N.Y.: Cornell University Press, 1988.

Brooks, Peter. *Body Work: Objects of Desire in Modern Narrative*. Cambridge: Harvard University Press.

Brown, J. "Reconstructing the Female Subject: Japanese Women Writers and the *Shishōsetsu*." *British Columbia Asian Review* 7 (Winter 1993-1994), 16-35.

Carroll, John. *Break-Out from the Crystal Palace: The anarcho-psychological critique: Stirner, Nietzsche, Dostoevsky*. London: Routledge and Kegan Paul, 1974.

Caws, Mary Ann. *The Poetry of Dada and Surrealism: Aragon, Breton, Tzara, Eluard and Desnos*. Princeton, N.J.: Princeton University Press, 1970.

Chadwick, Whitney. *Women Artists and the Surrealist Movement*. London: Thames and Hudson, 1985.

de Bary, Brett, trans. and ed. *Origins of Modern Japanese Literature*. By Karatani Kojin. Durham and London: Duke University Press, 1993.

Diprose, Rosalyn, and Robyn Ferrell, eds. *Cartographies: Poststructuralism and the mapping of bodies and spaces*. Sydney: Allen & Unwin, 1991.

Dodd, Elizabeth. *The Veiled Mirror and the Woman Poet*. Columbia, Missouri: University of Missouri Press, 1992.

Fowler, Edward. *The Rhetoric of Confession: Shishōsetsu in Early Twentieth Century Japanese Fiction*. Berkeley: University of California Press, 1988.

Friedman, Edward H. *The Antiheroine's Voice: Narrative Discourse and Transformations of the Picaresque*. Columbia, Missouri: University of Missouri Press, 1987.

Fujii, James A. *Complicit Fictions: The Subject in the Modern Japanese Prose Narrative*. Berkeley: University of California Press, 1993.

Gallop, Jane. *Thinking Through the Body*. New York: Columbia University Press, 1988.

Gilbert, Sandra M., and Susan Gubar. *No Man's Land: The Place of the Woman Writer in the Twentieth Century*. 2 vols. New Haven and London: Yale University Press, 1988.

Grosz, Elizabeth. *Volatile Bodies: Toward a Corporeal Feminism*. Bloomington and Indianapolis: Indiana University Press, 1994.

Hayashi Fumiko. *Homecoming*. Kaneko Hisakazu, trans. *Orient West* 8, no. 1 (May-June 1963): 48.

_____. *The Lord Buddha*. In *Women Poets of Japan* (formerly published as *The Burning Heart*, Seabury Press, 1977). Kenneth Rexroth, and Ikuko Atsumi, trans. and eds. New York: New Directions, 1982.

Hirsch, Marianne. *The Mother/Daughter Plot: Narrative, Psychoanalysis, Feminism*. Bloomington and Indianapolis: Indiana University Press, 1989.

Homans, Margaret. *Women Writers and Poetic Identity*. Princeton, N.J.: Princeton University Press, 1980.

Joll, James. *The Anarchists*. London: Methuen, 1964.

Kasulis, Thomas P., ed. *Self as Body in Asian Theory and Practice*. Albany: State University of New York Press, 1993.

Kery, Patricia Frantz. *Art Deco Graphics*. New York: Harry Abrams Inc., 1986.

Konishi Jin'ichi. "The Art of Renga." Trans. and introduction by Karen Brazell, and Lewis Cook. In *Journal of Japanese Studies* 2, no. 1 (Autumn 1975): 29-61.

Kono Ichirō, and Fukuda Rikutarō, trans. and eds. *An Anthology of Modern Japanese Poetry*. Tokyo: Kenkyūsha, 1957.

Lee, Sherman E. *Reflections of Reality in Japanese Art*. Cleveland: Cleveland Museum of Art, 1983.

Malm, William P. *Japanese Music and Musical Instruments*. Tokyo: Charles Tuttle, 1990.

Miner, Earl. *Japanese Linked Poetry*. Princeton, N.J.: Princeton University Press, 1979.

Morgan, Janice and Collette T . Hall, eds. *Gender and Genre in Literature: Redefining Autobiography in Twentieth Century Women's Fiction*. New York: Garland Publishing, 1991.

Nead, Lynda. "Getting down to basics: art, obscenity and the female nude." In *New Feminist Discourses: Critical Essays on Theories and Texts*. Isobel Armstrong, ed. London: Routledge, 1992.

Nolte, Sharon H., and Sally Ann Hastings. "The Meiji State's Policy Towards Women, 1890-1910." In *Recreating Japanese Women, 1600-1945*. Gail Bernstein, ed. Berkeley: University of California Press, 1991.

O'Grady, Lorraine. "Olympia's Maid: Reclaiming Black Female Subjectivity." In *New Feminist Criticism: Art, Identity, Action*. Joanna Frueh, Cassandra L. Langer, and Arlene Raven, eds. New York: Icon Editions, 1994.

Olney, James, ed. *Studies in Autobiography*. Oxford: Oxford University Press, 1988.

Personal Narratives Group. *Interpreting Women's Lives: Feminist Theory and Personal Narratives*. Bloomington: Indiana University Press, 1989.

Robinson, Sally Ann. *Gender and Self-Representation in Contemporary Women's Fiction*. Albany, New York: State University of New York Press, 1991.

Rubenstein, Roberta. *Boundaries of the Self: Gender, Culture, Fiction*. Urbana and Chicago: University of Illinois, 1987.

Schenck, Celeste. "All of a Piece: Women's Poetry and Autobiography." In *Life/Lines: Theorizing Women's Autobiography*. Bella Brodzski, and Celeste Schenck, eds. Ithaca, N.Y.: Cornell University Press, 1988.

Silverberg, Miriam: "The Modern Girl as Militant." In *Recreating Japanese Women, 1600-1945*. Gail Bernstein, ed. Berkeley: University of California Press, 1991.

Showalter, Elaine. "Feminist Criticism in the Wilderness." In *Modern Criticism and Theory*. David Lodge, ed. London and New York: Longman, 1988.

Smith, Sidonie. *A Poetics of Women's Autobiography: Marginality and the Fictions of Self-Representation*. Bloomington: Indiana University Press, 1987.

_____. *Subjectivity, Identity, and the Body: Women's Autobiographical Practice in the Twentieth Century*. Bloomington and Indianapolis: Indiana University Press, 1993.

_____ and Julia Watson, eds. *De/Colonizing the Subject: A Politics of Gender in Women's Autobiography*. Minneapolis: University of Minnesota Press, 1992.

Spence, Richard B. *Boris Savinkov: Renegade on the Left*. Boulder, Colorado: East European Monographs, Columbia University Press, 1991.

145

Spurling, Laurie. *Phenomenology and the Social World: The Philosophy of Merleau-Ponty and its Relation to the Social Sciences*. London: Routledge and Kegan Paul, 1977.

Stanley, Thomas A. *Ōsugi Sakae Anarchist in Taishō Japan: The Creativity of the Ego*. Honolulu: University of Hawaii Press, 1982.

Stanton, Domna C. *The Female Autograph*. New York: New York Literary Forum, 1984.

Torrance, Richard. *The Fiction of Tokuda Shūsei and the Emergence of Japan's New Middle Class*. Seattle: University of Washington Press, 1994.

Tsuzuki Chushichi. "Anarchism in Japan." In *Anarchism Today*. David E. Apter, and James Jolls, eds. London: Macmillan, 1971.

Uno, Kathleen, S. "Women and Changes in the Household Division of Labor." In *Recreating Japanese Women, 1600-1945*. Gail Bernstein, ed. Berkeley: University of California Press, 1991.

Watson, Julia. "Shadowed Presence: Modern Women Writers." In *Studies in Autobiography*. James Olney, ed. Oxford: Oxford University Press, 1988.

Wicks, Ulrich. *Picaresque Narrative, Picaresque Fictions*. Westport, Connecticut: Greenwood Press, 1989.

Willis, Sharon. *Marguerite Duras: Writing on the Body*. Urbana and Chicago: University of Chicago Press, 1987.

Yosano Akiko. *Tangled Hair: Selected Tanka from Midaregami*. Sanford Goldstein, and Seisha Shinoda, trans. Rutland, Vermont and Tokyo: Charles E. Tuttle, 1987.

Sources in Japanese

Adachi Ken'ichi. "Aouma wo mitari." In *General nihon bungaku arubamu 13: Hayashi Fumiko*. Adachi Ken'ichi, ed. Tokyo: Gakushū kenkyūsha, 1974.

Enchi Fumiko. "Aouma wo mitari' hyō." In *Nyonin geijutsu* 2, no. 8 (1929): 112.

Fukao Sumako. *Fukao Sumako senshū*. Tokyo: Shinjūsha, 1970.

Hagiwara Kyōjirō. *Hagiwara Kyōjirō shū*. In *Gendai nihon bungaku taikei*. Vol. 67, Tokyo: Chikuma shobō, 1973.

Hara Shiro, ed. *Kindai shi gendai shi hikkei*. Tokyo: Gakutosha, 1989.

Hayashi Fumiko. *Aouma wo mitari*. Tokyo: Nansō shoin, 1929. Reprint, Tokyo: Nihon kindai bungakukan, Horupu shuppan, 1981.

_____. *Aouma wo mitari*. In *Hayashi Fumiko zenshū*. Vol. 1, Tokyo: Shinchōsha, 1951.

_____. *Aouma wo mitari*. In *Hayashi Fumiko zenshū*. Vol. 1, Tokyo: Bunsendō, 1977.

_____. " 'Aouma wo mitari' kōki." In *Hayashi Fumiko zenshū*. Vol. 16, Tokyo: Bunsendō, 1977.

_____. "Bungakuteki jijoden." In *Hayashi Fumiko zenshū*. Vol. 10, Tokyo: Bunsendō, 1977.

148

_____ . *Hōrōki*. In *Hayashi Fumiko zenshū*. Vol. 2, Tokyo: Shinchōsha, 1951.

_____ . *Hōrōki*. In *Hayashi Fumiko zenshū*. Vol. 1, Tokyo: Bunsendō, 1977.

Hirabayashi Taiko. "Sehyō to kanojo—Hayashi Fumiko no tame ni." *Nyonin geijutsu* 2, no. 9 (1929): 66-67.

_____. *Hayashi Fumiko*. Tokyo: Shinchĥōsha, 1969.

_____. "Kaisetsu." In *Nihon no bungaku*. Vol. 47, Tokyo: Chūō kōronsha, 1970.

Ishikawa Sanshirō. "Aouma wo mitari jo." In *Aouma wo mitari*. Tokyo: Nansō shoin, 1929. Reprint, Tokyo: Nihon kindai bungakukan, Horupu shuppan, 1981.

Isogai Hideo. "Taishō kara Shōwa e." In *Shōwa no bungaku*. Tokyo: Yūseido, 1963.

_____. "Shōwa jūnendai no bungaku." In *Shōwa no bungaku*. Tokyo: Yūseido, 1963.

_____. "Hyōden." In *Shinchōsha nihon bungaku arubamu: Hayashi Fumiko 34*. Tokyo: Shinchōsha, 1986.

Itagaki Naoko. *Fujin sakka hyoden*. Tokyo: Nihon tōsho sentaa, 1987.

_____. "Hayashi Fumiko." *Kokubungaku kaishaku to kanshō* (March 1972): 101-104.

_____. *Hayashi Fumiko: gendai no esupuri*. Tokyo: Shibundō, 1965.

_____. *Hayashi Fumiko no shōgai: uzushio no jinsei*. Tokyo: Daiwa shobō, 1966.

Itō Shinkichi. "Hagiwara Kyōjirō—shi ni okeru shisō no taiken." In *Gendai nihon bungaku taikei*. Vol. 67, Tokyo: Chikuma shobō, 1973.

Kawai Michiko. "Hayashi Fumiko—Onna no seikatsu no ba ni tsuite." In *Jōryu bungei kenkyū*. Mawatani Kenzaburō, ed. Tokyo: Nansōsha, 1973.

Kihara Koichi. *Nihon no shi: nihon no shi no nagare*. Tokyo: Horupu shuppan, 1975.

Mori Eiichi. *Hayashi Fumiko no keisei—sono sei to hyōgen*. Tokyo: Yūseido, 1992.

Muramatsu Sadataka. "Hayashi Fumiko." In *Nihon joryu bungaku shi*. Vol. 2, Yoshida Seiichi, ed. Tokyo: Dobun shoin, 1969.

_____. "Mazushisa no naka kara no kaika: Hayashi Fumiko." In *Kindai joryū sakka no shōzō*. Tokyo: Tōsho sensho, 1980.

Nakamura Mitsuo. "Hayashi Fumiko ron." In *Gendai nihon bungaku taikei*. Vol. 69, Tokyo: Chikuma shobō, 1969.

Nojima Hidekatsu. "Hayashi Fumiko: hito to sakuhin." In *Shōwa bungaku zenshū*. Vol. 8, Tokyo: Shōgakkan, 1988.

Nomura Kichiya. *Sankakukei no taiyō* (selections). In *Nihon gendaishi taikei*. Vol. 8. Tokyo: Kawade shobō, 1951.

Odagiri Hideo. "Sakuhin kaisetsu." In *Nihon gendai bungaku zenshū*. Vol. 78, Tokyo: Kodansha, 1967.

Ogata Akiko. *Nyonin geijutsu no hitobito*. Tokyo: Domesu shuppan, 1981.

_____. *Nyonin geijutsu no sekai*. Tokyo: Domesu shuppan, 1980.

Okamoto Jun. *Yoru kara asa e* (selections). In *Nihon gendai shi taikei*. Vol. 8, Tokyo: Kawade shobō, 1951.

Setouchi Harumi. "Hōrōki to Hayashi Fumiko." In *Meisaku no naka no onnatachi*. Tokyo: Kadokawa shoten, 1984.

Takahashi Shinkichi. *Dadaisuto Shinkichi no shi*. In *Gendai nihon bungaku taikei*. Vol. 67, Tokyo: Chikuma shobō, 1973.

Takami Jun. "Zen josei shinshutsu kōshinkyoku—Hayashi Fumiko Hōrōki." In *Shōwa bungaku seisui shi*. Tokyo: Kodansha, 1965.

Takemoto Chimakichi. *Ningen Hayashi Fumiko*. Tokyo: Chikuma shobō, 1985.

Tokuda Kazuho. "Fumiko to Shūsei." In *Chikuma gendai bungaku taikei*. Vol. 39 (Geppō 66), Tokyo: Chikuma shobō, 1975.

Tōmaru Tatsu. "Umoreta shijin no shōzō," In *Gendai shi bunko: Hayashi Fumiko shishū 1026*. Tokyo: Shichōsha, 1984.

Tsuboi Sakae and Hirabayashi Taiko. "Hayashi Fumiko no omoide." In *Nihon no bungaku 47: Hayashi Fumiko geppō*, July, 1964. Reprint in *Gendai shi bunko: Hayashi Fumiko shishū 1026*. Tokyo: Shichōsha, 1984.

Tsuboi Shigeji. "Mumei jidai no Hayashi Fumiko ." In *Shinchō nihon bungaku 22: Hayashi Fumiko geppō*, September, 1971. Reprint in *Gendai shi bunko: Hayashi Fumiko shishū 1026*. Tokyo: Shichōsha, 1984.

_____. *Tsuboi Shegeji shishū*. In *Nihon gendaishi taikei*. Vol. 8, Tokyo: Kawade shobō, 1951.

Tsuji Jun. "Jo." In *Aouma wo mitari*. Tokyo: Nansō shoin, 1929. Reprint, Tokyo: Nihon kindai bungakukan, 1981.

Tsuruoka Yoshihisa, ed. *Nihon no shi: Shōwa no shi I* (Vol. 2, part 1), Tokyo: Horupu shuppan, 1975.

Wada Yoshie. "Hayashi Fumiko to sono jidai." In *Gendai nihon bungaku arubamu 13: Hayashi Fumiko*. Tokyo: Gakushū kenkyūsha, 1974.

_____. "Kaisetsu." In *Hayashi Fumiko shū: gendai no bungaku 17*. Tokyo: Kawade shobō shinsha, 1965.

_____. "Kaisetsu." In *Hayashi Fumiko shū: shinchō nihon bungaku 22*. Tokyo: Shinchōsha, 1973.

Yamada Yusaku. *Joryū bungaku no genzai*. Tokyo: Gakujutsu tosho, 1985.

Yamamoto Kenkichi. "Hayashi Fumiko." In *Chikuma gendai bungaku taikei.* Vol. 39, Tokyo: Chikuma shobō, 1975.

Yosano Akiko. *Midaregami.* In *Nihon kindai bungaku taikei.* Vol. 17, Tokyo: Kadokawa shoten, 1969.

CORNELL EAST ASIA SERIES

FORTHCOMING

To order, please contact the Cornell East Asia Series, East Asia Program,
Cornell University, 140 Uris Hall, Ithaca, NY 14853-7601, USA; phone
(607) 255-6222, fax (607) 255-1388, internet: kks3@cornell.edu.

I Saw a Pale Horse
AND SELECTED POEMS FROM
Diary of a Vagabond

HAYASHI FUMIKO, one of the most popular prose writers of the Showa
era, began writing as a down-and-out poet wandering the streets of 1920s
Tokyo. In these translations of her first poetry collection, *I Saw a Pale
Horse*, and selected poems from *Diary of a Vagabond*, Fumiko's literary
origins are colorfully revealed. Little known in the west, these early poetic
texts focus on Fumiko's unconventional early life, and her construction of
a female subject that would challenge, with gusto and panache, accepted
notions not only of class, family, and gender but also of female poetic
practice.

JANICE BROWN is Assistant Professor of modern Japanese literature at the
University of Alberta, Edmonton, Canada. She has written a variety of
articles on modern Japanese writers, including Hayashi Fumiko. Her
present research interests include Japanese women's poetry and autobiog-
raphy.

3-97/.5M paper/.2M cloth/BB